THE DOW LOW DROP

ROY FISHER

The Dow Low Drop

NEW & SELECTED POEMS

BLOODAXE BOOKS

ISBN: 1 85224 340 6

First published 1996 by
Bloodaxe Books Ltd,
P.O. Box 1SN,
Newcastle upon Tyne NE99 1SN.

Bloodaxe Books Ltd acknowledges
the financial assistance of Northern Arts.

Cover printing by J. Thomson Colour Printers Ltd, Glasgow.

Printed in Great Britain by
Cromwell Press Ltd, Broughton Gifford, Melksham, Wiltshire.

To Ben & Joe Fisher

Acknowledgements

This edition includes poems selected from Roy Fisher's previous books: *City* (Migrant Press, 1961), *Ten Interiors with Various Figures* (Tarasque Press, 1966), *The Ship's Orchestra* (Fulcrum Press, 1966), *Collected Poems* (Fulcrum Press, 1968), *Matrix* and *The Cut Pages* (both Fulcrum Press, 1971), *The Thing About Joe Sullivan: Poems 1971-1977* (Carcanet, 1978), *Poems 1955-1980* (Oxford University Press, 1980), and *A Furnace* (Oxford University Press, 1986). The poems from *Poems 1979-1987* are taken from a section of new work in *Poems 1955-1987* (Oxford University Press, 1988). All these books are out of print.

For work in the *New & Uncollected Poems* section of this book, acknowledgements are due to Pig Press for the pamphlet *It Follows That* (1994); passages from *The Dow Low Drop* first appeared in *Durham Review*, and 'Hand-Me-Downs' in *Klaonica: poems for Bosnia* (Bloodaxe Books/*The Independent*, 1993).

This new selection of Roy Fisher's poetry does not cover his most recent collection *Birmingham River* (1994), which is available from Oxford University Press

Contents

CITY
(1961)

On one of the steep slopes that rise towards the centre of the city all the buildings have been destroyed within the past year: a whole district of the tall narrow houses that spilled around what were a hundred years ago outlying factories has gone. The streets remain, among the rough quadrilaterals of brick rubble, veering awkwardly towards one another through nothing; at night their rounded surfaces still shine under the irregularly-set gaslamps, and tonight they dully reflect also the yellowish flare, diffused and baleful, that hangs flat in the clouds a few hundred feet above the city's invisible heart. Occasional cars move cautiously across this waste, as if suspicious of the emptiness; there is little to separate the roadways from what lies between them. Their tail-lights vanish slowly into the blocks of surrounding buildings, maybe a quarter of a mile from the middle of the desolation.

And what is it that lies between these purposeless streets? There is not a whole brick, a foundation to stumble across, a drainpipe, a smashed fowlhouse; the entire place has been razed flat, dug over, and smoothed down again. The bald curve of the hillside shows quite clearly here, near its crown, where the brilliant road, stacked close on either side with warehouses and shops, runs out towards the west. Down below, the district that fills the hollow is impenetrably black. The streets there are so close and so twisted among their massive tenements that it is impossible to trace the line of a single one of them by its lights. The lamps that can be seen shine oddly, and at mysterious distances, as if they were in a marsh. Only the great flat-roofed factory shows clear by its bulk, stretching across three or four whole blocks just below the edge of the waste, with solid rows of lit windows.

Lullaby and Exhortation for the Unwilling Hero

A fish,
Firelight,
A watery ceiling:
Under the door
The drunk wind sleeps.

The bell in the river,
The loaf half eaten,
The coat of the sky.

A pear,
Perfume,
A white glade of curtains:
Out in the moonlight
The smoke reaches high.

The statue in the cellar,
The skirt on the chairback,
The throat of the street.

A shell,
Shadow,
A floor spread with silence:
Faint on the skylight
The fat moths beat.

The pearl in the stocking,
The coals left to die,
The bell in the river,
The loaf half eaten,
The coat of the sky.

The night slides like a thaw
And oil-drums bang together.

A frosted-glass door opening, then another.
Orange and blue *décor.*
The smoke that hugs the ceiling tastes of pepper.

What steps descend, what rails conduct?
Sodium bulbs equivocate,
And cowls of ventilators
With limewashed breath hint at the places
To which the void lift cages plunge or soar.

Prints on the landing walls
Are all gone blind with steam;
A voice under the floor
Swings a dull axe against a door.
The gaping office block of night
Shudders into the deep sky overhead:

Thrust down your foot in sleep
Among its depths. Do not respect
The janitors in bed,
The balustrades of iron bars,
The gusty stairwells; thrust it deep,
Into a concrete garage out of sight,
And rest among the cars
That, shut in filtered moonlight,
Sweat mercury and lead.

Subway trains, or winds of indigo,
Bang oil-drums in the yard for war:
Already, half-built towers
Over the bombed city
Show mouths that soon will speak no more,
Stoppered with the perfections of tomorrow.

You can lie women in your bed
With glass and mortar in their hair.
Pocket the key, and draw the curtains,
They'll not care.

Letters on a sweetshop window:
At last the rain slides them askew,
The foetus in the dustbin moves one claw.

And from the locomotive
That's halted on the viaduct
A last white rag of steam
Blows ghostly across the gardens.
When you wake, what will you do?

Under the floorboards of your dream
Gun barrels rolled in lint
Jockey the rooms this way and that.
Across the suburbs, squares of colour gleam:
Swaddled in pink and apricot,
The people are 'making love'.

Those are bright points that flicker
Softly, and vanish one by one.
Your telegraphic fingers mutter the world.
What will they reach for when your sleep is done?

The hiss of tyres along the gutter,
Odours of polish in the air;
A car sleeps in the neighbouring room,
A wardrobe by its radiator.

The rumbling canisters beat for you
Who are a room now altogether bare,
An open mouth pressed outwards against life,
Tasting the sleepers' breath,
The palms of hands, discarded shoes,
Lilac wood, the blade of a breadknife.

Before dawn in the sidings,
Over whose even tracks
Fat cooling towers caress the sky,
The rows of trucks
Extend: black, white,
White, grey, white, black,
Black, white, black, grey,
Marshalled like building blocks:
Women are never far away.

In the century that has passed since this city has become great, it
has twice laid itself out in the shape of a wheel. The ghost of the
older one still lies among the spokes of the new, those dozen high-
ways that thread constricted ways through the inner suburbs, then
thrust out, twice as wide, across the housing estates and into the
countryside, dragging moraines of buildings with them. Sixty or
seventy years ago there were other main roads, quite as important
as these were then, but lying between their paths. By day they are

simply alternatives, short cuts, lined solidly with parked cars and crammed with delivery vans. They look merely like side-streets, heartlessly overblown in some excess of Victorian expansion. By night, or on a Sunday, you can see them for what they are. They are still lit meagrely, and the long rows of houses, three and four storeys high, rear black above the lamps enclosing the road-ways, clamping them off from whatever surrounds them. From these pavements you can sometimes see the sky at night, not obscured as it is in most parts of the city by the greenish-blue haze of light that steams out of the mercury vapour lamps. These streets are not worth lighting. The houses have not been turned into shops – they are not villas either that might have become offices, but simply tall dwellings, opening straight off the street, with cavernous entries leading into back courts.

The people who live in them are mostly very old. Some have lived through three wars, some through only one; wars of newspapers, of mysterious sciences, of coercion, of disappearance. Wars that have come down the streets from the unknown city and the unknown world, like rainwater floods in the gutters. There are small shops at street corners, with blank rows of houses between them; and taverns carved only shallowly into the massive walls. When these people go into the town, the buses they travel in stop just before they reach it, in the sombre back streets behind the Town Hall and the great insurance offices.

These lost streets are decaying only very slowly. The impacted lives of their inhabitants, the meaninglessness of news, the dead black of the chimney breasts, the conviction that the wind itself comes only from the next street, all wedge together to keep destruction out; to deflect the eye of the developer. And when destruction comes, it is total: the printed notices on the walls, block by block, a few doors left open at night, broken windows advancing down a street until fallen slates appear on the pavement and are not kicked away. Then, after a few weeks of this, the machines arrive.

The Entertainment of War

I saw the garden where my aunt had died
And her two children and a woman from next door;
It was like a burst pod filled with clay.

A mile away in the night I had heard the bombs
Sing and then burst themselves between cramped houses
With bright soft flashes and sounds like banging doors;

The last of them crushed the four bodies into the ground,
Scattered the shelter, and blasted my uncle's corpse
Over the housetop and into the street beyond.

Now the garden lay stripped and stale; the iron shelter
Spread out its separate petals around a smooth clay saucer,
Small, and so tidy it seemed nobody had ever been there.

When I saw it, the house was blown clean by blast and care:
Relations had already torn out the new fireplaces;
My cousin's pencils lasted me several years.

And in his office notepad that was given me
I found solemn drawings in crayon of blondes without dresses.
In his lifetime I had not known him well.

Those were the things I noticed at ten years of age:
Those, and the four hearses outside our house,
The chocolate cakes, and my classmates' half-shocked envy.

But my grandfather went home from the mortuary
And for five years tried to share the noises in his skull,
Then he walked out and lay under a furze-bush to die.

When my father came back from identifying the daughter
He asked us to remind him of her mouth.
We tried. He said 'I think it was the one'.

These were marginal people I had met only rarely
And the end of the whole household meant that no grief was seen;
Never have people seemed so absent from their own deaths.

This bloody episode of four whom I could understand better dead
Gave me something I needed to keep a long story moving;
I had no pain of it; can find no scar even now.

But had my belief in the fiction not been thus buoyed up
I might, in the sigh and strike of the next night's bombs
Have realised a little what they meant, and for the first time been
        afraid.

North Area

Those whom I love avoid all mention of it,
Though certain gestures they've in common
Persuade me they know it well:
A place where I can never go.

No point in asking why, or why not.
I picture it, though
There must be dunes with cement walks,
A twilight of aluminium
Among beach huts and weather-stained handrails;
Much glass to reflect the clouds;
And a glint of blood in the cat-ice that holds the rushes.

The edge of the city. A low hill with houses on one side and rough
common land on the other, stretching down to where a dye-works
lies along the valley road. Pithead gears thrust out above the haw-
thorn bushes; everywhere prefabricated workshops jut into the
fields and the allotments. The society of singing birds and the
society of mechanical hammers inhabit the world together, slightly
ruffled and confined by each other's presence.

By the Pond

This is bitter enough: the pallid water
With yellow rushes crowding toward the shore,
That fishermen's shack.

The pit-mound's taut and staring wire fences,
The ashen sky. All these can serve as conscience.
For the rest, I'll live.

Brick-dust in sunlight. That is what I see now in the city, a dry epic flavour, whose air is human breath. A place of walls made straight with plumbline and trowel, to dessicate and crumble in the sun and smoke. Blistered paint on cisterns and girders, cracking to show the priming. Old men spit on the paving slabs, little boys urinate; and the sun dries it as it dries out patches of damp on plaster facings to leave misshapen stains. I look for things here that make old men and dead men seem young. Things which have escaped, the landscapes of many childhoods.

Wharves, the oldest parts of factories, tarred gable ends rearing to take the sun over lower roofs. Soot, sunlight, brick-dust; and the breath that tastes of them.

At the time when the great streets were thrust out along the old high-roads and trackways, the houses shouldering towards the country and the back streets filling in the widening spaces between them like webbed membranes, the power of will in the town was more open, less speciously democratic, than it is now. There were, of course, cottage railway stations, a jail that pretended to be a castle out of Grimm, public urinals surrounded by screens of cast-iron lacework painted green and scarlet; but there was also an arrogant ponderous architecture that dwarfed and terrified the people by its sheer size and functional brutality: the workhouses and the older hospitals, the thick-walled abattoir, the long vaulted market-halls, the striding canal bridges and railway viaducts. Brunel was welcome here. Compared with these structures the straight white blocks and concrete roadways of today are a fairground, a clear dream just before waking, the creation of salesmen rather than of engineers. The new city is bred out of a hard will, but as it appears, it shows itself a little ingratiating, a place of arcades, passages, easy ascents, good light. The eyes twinkle, beseech and veil themselves; the full, hard mouth, the broad jaw – these are no longer made visible to all.

A street half a mile long with no buildings, only a continuous embankment of sickly grass along one side, with railway signals on it, and strings of trucks through whose black-spoked wheels you can see the sky; and for the whole length of the other a curving wall of bluish brick, caked with soot and thirty feet high. In it, a few wicket gates painted ochre, and fingermarked, but never open. Cobbles in the roadway.

A hundred years ago this was almost the edge of town. The goods yards, the gasworks and the coal stores were established on tips and hillocks in the sparse fields that lay among the houses. Between this place and the centre, a mile or two up the hill, lay a continuous huddle of low streets and courts, filling the marshy valley of the meagre river that now flows under brick and tarmac. And this was as far as the railway came, at first. A great station was built, towering and stony. The sky above it was southerly. The stately approach, the long curves of wall, still remain, but the place is a goods depot with most of its doors barred and pots of geraniums at those windows that are not shuttered. You come upon it suddenly in its open prospect out of tangled streets of small factories. It draws light to itself, especially at sunset, standing still and smooth faced, looking westwards at the hill. I am not able to imagine the activity that must once have been here. I can see no ghosts of men and women, only the gigantic ghost of stone. They are too frightened of it to pull it down.

The Sun Hacks

The sun hacks at the slaughterhouse campanile,
And by the butchers' cars, packed tail-to-kerb,
Masks under white caps wake into human faces.

The river shudders as dawn drums on its culvert;
On the first bus nightworkers sleep, or stare
At hoardings that look out on yesterday.

The whale-back hill assumes its concrete city:
The white-flanked towers, the stillborn monuments;
The thousand golden offices, untenanted.

At night on the station platform, near a pile of baskets, a couple embraced, pressed close together and swaying a little. It was hard to see where the girl's feet and legs were. The suspicion this aroused soon caused her hands, apparently joined behind her lover's back, to become a small brown paper parcel under the arm of a stout engine-driver who leaned, probably drunk, against the baskets, his cap so far forward as almost to conceal his face. I could not banish the thought that what I had first seen was in fact his own androgynous fantasy, the self-sufficient core of his stupor. Such a romantic thing, so tender, for him to contain. He looked more comic and complaisant than the couple had done, and more likely to fall heavily to the floor.

A café with a frosted glass door through which much light is diffused. A tall young girl comes out and stands in front of it, her face and figure quite obscured by this milky radiance.

She treads out on to a lopsided ochre panel of lit pavement before the doorway and becomes visible as a coloured shape, moving sharply. A wrap of honey and ginger, a flared saffron skirt, grey-white shoes. She goes off past the Masonic Temple with a young man: he is pale, with dark hair and a shrunken, earnest face. You could imagine him a size larger. Just for a moment, as it happens, there is no one else in the street at all. Their significance escapes rapidly like a scent, before the footsteps vanish among the car engines.

A man in the police court. He looked dapper and poker-faced, his arms straight, the long fingers just touching the hem of his checked jacket. Four days after being released from the prison where he had served two years for theft he had been discovered at midnight clinging like a tree-shrew to the bars of a glass factory-roof. He made no attempt to explain his presence there; the luminous nerves that made him fly up to it were not visible in daylight, and the police seemed hardly able to believe this was the creature they had brought down in the darkness.

In this city the governing authority is limited and mean: so limited that it can do no more than preserve a superficial order. It supplies fuel, water and power. It removes a fair proportion of the refuse, cleans the streets after a fashion, and discourages fighting. With these things, and a few more of the same sort, it is content. This could never be a capital city for all its size. There is no mind in it, no regard. The sensitive, the tasteful, the fashionable, the intolerant and powerful, have not moved through it as they have moved through London, evaluating it, altering it deliberately, setting in motion wars of feeling about it. Most of it has never been seen.

In an afternoon of dazzling sunlight in the thronged streets, I saw at first no individuals but a composite monster, its unfeeling surfaces matted with dust: a mass of necks, limbs without extremities, trunks without heads; unformed stirrings and shovings spilling across the streets it had managed to get itself provided with.

Later, as the air cooled, flowing loosely about the buildings that stood starkly among the declining rays, the creature began to divide and multiply. At crossings I could see people made of straws, rags, cartons, the stuffing of burst cushions, kitchen refuse. Outside the Grand Hotel, a long-boned carrot-haired girl with glasses, loping along, and with strips of bright colour, rich, silky green and blue, in her soft clothes. For a person made of such scraps she was beautiful.

Faint blue light dropping down through the sparse leaves of the plane trees in the churchyard opposite after sundown, cooling and shaping heads, awakening eyes.

The Hill behind the Town

Sullen hot noon, a loop of wire,
With zinc light standing everywhere,
A glint on the chapels,
Glint on the chapels.

Under my heel a loop of wire
Dragged in the dust is earth's wide eye,
Unseen for days,
Unseen days.

Geranium-wattled, fenced in wire,
Caged white cockerels crowd near
And stretch red throats,
Stretch red throats;

Their cries tear grievous through taut wire,
Drowned in tanks of factory sirens
At sullen noon,
Sullen hot noon.

The day's on end; a loop of wire
Kicked from the dust's bleak daylight leaves
A blind white world,
Blind white world.

The Poplars

Where the road divides
Just out of town
By the wall beyond the filling-station
Four Lombardy poplars
Brush stiff against the moorland wind.

Clarity is in their tops
That no one can touch
Till they are felled,
Brushwood to cart away:

To know these tall pointers
I need to withdraw
From what is called my life
And from my net
Of achievable desires.

Why should their rude and permanent virginity
So capture me? Why should studying
These lacunae of possibility
Relax the iron templates of obligation
Leaving me simply Man?

All I have done, or can do
Is prisoned in its act:
I think I am afraid of becoming
A cemetery of performance.

Starting to Make a Tree

First we carried out the faggot of steel stakes; they varied in length, though most were taller than a man.

We slid one free of the bundle and drove it into the ground, first padding the top with rag, that the branch might not be injured with leaning on it.

Then we took turns to choose stakes of the length we wanted, and to feel for the distances between them. We gathered to thrust them firmly in.

There were twenty or thirty of them in all; and when they were in place we had, round the clearing we had left for the trunk, an ir-regular radial plantation of these props, each with its wad of white at the tip. It was to be an old, downcurving tree.

This was in keeping with the burnt, chemical blue of the soil, and the even hue of the sky which seemed to have been washed with a pale brownish smoke;

another clue was the flatness of the horizon on all sides except the north, where it was broken by the low slate or tarred shingle roofs of the houses, which stretched away from us for a mile or more.

This was the work of the morning. It was done with care, for we had no wish to make revisions;

we were, nonetheless, a little excited, and hindered the women at their cooking in our anxiety to know whose armpit and whose groin would help us most in the modelling of the bole, and the thrust of the boughs.

That done, we spent the early dusk of the afternoon gathering mat-erials from the nearest houses; and there was plenty:

a great flock mattress; two carved chairs; cement; chicken-wire; tarpaulin; a smashed barrel; lead piping; leather of all kinds; and many small things.

In the evening we sat late, and discussed how we could best use them. Our tree was to be very beautiful.

Yet whenever I see that some of these people around me are bodily in love, I feel it is my own energy, my own hope, tension and sense of time in hand, that have gathered and vanished down that dark drain; it is I who am left, shivering and exhausted, to try and kick the lid back into place so that I can go on without the fear of being able to feel only vertically, like a blind wall, or thickly, like the tyres of a bus.

Lovers turn to me faces of innocence where I would expect wariness. They have disappeared for entire hours into the lit holes of life, instead of lying stunned on its surface as I, and so many, do for so long; or instead of raising their heads cautiously and scenting the manifold airs that blow through the streets.

The city asleep. In it there are shadows that are sulphurous, tanks of black bile. The glitter on the roadways is the deceptive ore that shines on coal.

The last buses have left the centre; the pallid faces of the crowd looked like pods, filled by a gusty summer that had come too late for plenty.

Silvered rails that guide pedestrians at street corners stand useless. Towards midnight, or at whatever hour the sky descends with its full iron weight, the ceilings drop lower everywhere; each light is partial, and proper only to its place. There is no longer any general light, only particular lights that overlap.

Out of the swarming thoroughfares, the night makes its own streets with a rake that drags persuaded people out of its way: streets where the bigger buildings have already swung themselves round to odd angles against the weakened currents of the traffic.

There are lamplit streets where the full darkness is only in the deep drains and in the closed eyesockets and shut throats of the old as they lie asleep; their breath moves red tunnel-lights.

The main roads hold their white-green lights with difficulty, like long, loaded boughs; when the machines stop moving down them their gradients reappear.

Journeys at night: sometimes grooves in a thick substance, sometimes raised weals on black skin.

The city at night has no eye, any more than it has by day, although you would expect to find one; and over much of it the sleep is aqueous and incomplete, like that of a hospital ward.

But to some extent it stops, drops and congeals. It could be broken like asphalt, and the men and women rolled out like sleeping maggots.

Once I wanted to prove the world was sick. Now I want to prove it healthy. The detection of sickness means that death has established itself as an element of the timetable; it has come within the range of the measurable. Where there is no time there is no sickness.

The Wind at Night

The suburb lies like a hand tonight,
A man's thick hand, so stubborn
No child or poet can move it.

The wind drives itself mad with messages,
Clattering train wheels over the roofs,
Collapsing streets of sound until
Far towers, daubed with swollen light,
Lunge closer to abuse it,

This suburb like a sleeping hand,
With helpless elms that shudder
Angry between its fingers,
Powerless to disprove it.

And, although the wind derides
The spaces of this stupid quarter,
And sets the time of night on edge,
It mocks the hand, but cannot lose it:

This stillness keeps us in the flesh,
For us to use it.

I stare into the dark; and see a window, a large sash window of four panes, such as might be found in the living-room of any fair-sized old house. Its curtains are drawn back and it looks out on to a small damp garden, narrow close at hand where the kitchen and outhouses lead back, and then almost square. Privet and box surround it, and the flowerbeds are empty save for a few laurels or rhododendrons, some leafless rose shrubs and a giant yucca. It is a December afternoon, and it is raining. Not far from the window is a black marble statue of a long-haired, long-bearded old man. His robes are conventionally archaic, and he sits, easily enough, on what seems a pile of small boulders, staring intently and with a look of great intelligence towards the patch of wall just under the kitchen window. The statue looks grimy, but its exposed surfaces are highly polished by the rain, so that the nose and the cheek-bones stand out strongly in the gloom. It is rather smaller than life-size. It is clearly not in its proper place: resting as it does across the moss of the raised border, it is appreciably tilted forward and to one side, almost as if it had been abandoned as too heavy by those who were trying to move it – either in or out.

Walking through the suburb at night, as I pass the dentist's house I hear a clock chime a quarter, a desolate brassy sound. I know where it stands, on the mantelpiece in the still surgery. The chime falls back into the house, and beyond it, without end. Peace.

I sense the simple nakedness of these tiers of sleeping men and women beneath whose windows I pass. I imagine it in its own setting, a mean bathroom in a house no longer new, a bathroom with plank panelling, painted a peculiar shade of green by an amateur, and badly preserved. It is full of steam, so much as to obscure the yellow light and hide the high, patched ceiling. In this dream, standing quiet, the private image of the householder or his wife, damp and clean.

I see this as it might be floating in the dark, as if the twinkling point of a distant street-lamp had blown in closer, swelling and softening to a foggy oval. I can call up a series of such glimpses that need have no end, for they are all the bodies of strangers. Some are deformed or diseased, some are ashamed, but the peace of humility and weakness is there in them all.

I have often felt myself to be vicious, in living so much by the eye, yet among so many people. I can be afraid that the egg of light through which I see these bodies might present itself as a keyhole. Yet I can find no sadism in the way I see them now. They are warm-fleshed, yet their shapes have the minuscule, remote morality of some mediaeval woodcut of the Expulsion: an eternally startled Adam, a permanently bemused Eve. I see them as homunculi, moving privately each in a softly lit fruit in a nocturnal tree. I can consider without scorn or envy the well-found bedrooms I pass, walnut and rose-pink, altars of tidy, dark-haired women, bare-backed, wifely. Even in these I can see order.

I come quite often now upon a sort of ecstasy, a rag of light blowing among the things I know, making me feel I am not the one for whom it was intended, that I have inadvertently been looking through another's eyes and have seen what I cannot receive.

I want to believe I live in a single world. That is why I am keeping my eyes at home while I can. The light keeps on separating the world like a table knife: it sweeps across what I see and suggests what I do not. The imaginary comes to me with as much force as the real, the remembered with as much force as the immediate. The countries on the map divide and pile up like ice-flocs: what is strange is that I feel no stress, no grating discomfort among the confusion, no loss; only a belief that I should not be here. I see the iron fences and the shallow ditches of the countryside the mild wind has travelled over. I cannot enter that countryside; nor can I escape it. I cannot join together the mild wind and the shallow ditches, I cannot lay the light across the world and then watch it slide away. Each thought is at once translucent and icily capricious. A polytheism without gods.

The Park

If you should go there on such a day –
The red sun disappearing,
Netted behind black sycamores;

If you should go there on such a day –
The sky drawn thin with frost,
Its cloud-rims bright and bitter –

If you should go there on such a day,
Maybe the old goose will chase you away.

If you should go there to see
The shallow concrete lake,
Scummed over, fouled with paper;

If you should go there to see
The grass plots, featureless,
Muddy, and bruised, and balding –

If you should go there to see,
Maybe the old goose will scare you as he scared me,

Waddling fast on his diseased feet,
His orange bill thrust out,
His eyes indignant;

Waddling fast on his diseased feet,
His once ornamental feathers
Baggy, and smeared with winter –

Waddling fast on his diseased feet,
The old goose will one day reach death; and be unfit to eat.

And when the goose is dead, then we
Can say we're able, at last,
No longer hindered from going;

And when the goose is dead, then we
Have the chance, if we still want it,
To wander the park at leisure;

– Oh, when excuse is dead, then we
Must visit there, most diligently.

TEN INTERIORS WITH
VARIOUS FIGURES

(1966)

Interiors with Various Figures

1 *Experimenting*

Experimenting, experimenting,
With long damp fingers twisting all the time and in the dusk
White like unlit electric bulbs she said
'This green goes with this purple,' the hands going,
The question pleased: 'Agree?'

Squatting beside a dark brown armchair just round from the
       fireplace, one hand on a coalscuttle the other prickling
       across the butchered remains of my hair,
I listen to the nylon snuffle in her poking hands,
Experimenting, experimenting.
'Old sexy-eyes,' is all I say.

So I have to put my face into her voice, a shiny baize-lined
       canister that says all round me, staring in:
'I've tried tonight. This place!' Experimenting. And I:
'The wind off the wallpaper blows your hair bigger.'

Growing annoyed, I think, she clouds over, reminds me she's a
       guest, first time here, a comparative stranger, however
       close; 'Doesn't *welcome* me.' She's not young, of course;
Trying it on, though, going on about the milk bottle, tableleg,
The little things. Oh, a laugh somewhere. More words.
She knows I don't *live* here.

Only a little twilight is left washing around outside, her unease
       interfering with it as I watch.
Silence. Maybe some conversation. I begin:
'Perhaps you've had a child secretly sometime?'

'Hm?' she says, closed up. The fingers start again, exploring up
       and down and prodding, smoothing. Carefully
She asks 'At least – why can't you have more walls?'
Really scared. I see she means it.

To comfort her I say how there's one wall each, they can't
        outnumber us, walls, lucky to have the one with the
        lightswitch, our situation's better than beyond the
        backyard, where indeed the earth seems to stop pretty
        abruptly and not restart;
Then she says, very finely:
'I can't look,' and 'Don't remind me,' and 'That blue gulf'.

So I ask her to let her fingers do the white things again and let
        her eyes look and her hair blow bigger, all in the dusk
        deeper and the coloured stuffs audible and odorous;
But she shuts her eyes big and mutters:
                'And when the moon with horror −
                And when the moon with horror −
                And when the moon with horror −'
So I say 'Comes blundering blind up the side tonight'.
She: 'We hear it bump and scrape'.
I: 'We hear it giggle'. Looks at me,
'And when the moon with horror,' she says.

Squatting beside a dark brown armchair just round from the
        fireplace, one hand on a coalscuttle the other prickling
        across the butchered remains of my hair,
'What have you been reading, then?' I ask her,
Experimenting, experimenting.

2 *The Small Room*

Why should I let him shave the hairs from me? I hardly know him.

Of all the rooms, this is a very small room.

I cannot tell if it was he who painted the doors this colour; himself
        who lit the fire just before I arrived.

That bulb again. It has travelled even here.

In the corner, a cupboard where evidently a dog sleeps. The
        preparations are slow.

He is allowed to buy the same sort of electricity as everybody else,
      but his shirt, his milk bottle, his electricity resemble one
      another more than they resemble others of their kind.
      A transformation at his door, at his voice, under his eye.

This will include me too; yet I hardly know him. Not well enough
      to be sure which excuses would make him let me go, now,
      at once.

Shave the hairs from my body. Which of us thought of this thing?

3 *The Lampshade*

It is globed
      and like white wax.
Someone left it
      on the table corner
under the lamp-holder with the stiff ring.

Across its curve
      a few red strands stick.
Just now she wrapped her hair around
to stage an interview with it.
Inside the hair.

Now, beside the cupboard,
      skirt pulled down,
she sits on the floor
watching me
      through brass eyes.

Thinking what she told the lampshade,
      what it volunteered,
the moist globe in her hair.

Soon she'll stand up.
She helps me make the bed and gets us
brownish wet food about this time.

The white globe stays with us
at mealtimes.

4 *The Steam Crane*

Before breakfast you drew down the blind.

Soon it will be afternoon outside. Hear the steam crane start up
    again

Deep in the world.

You sprawl with no shoes, wet with something from the floor
    you didn't see in the dark.

Black skirt. Black hair. Nothing troubles you, you big shadow.
    Much time has fallen away.

Wearing a blanket I sit in a hard armchair, a jug at my feet.

There's nothing I can give you as beautiful as the flowers on the
    wallpaper.

Under the wallpaper, plaster, bonded with black hairs.

5 *The Wrestler*

Stripped more or less, they wrestle among the furniture on his
    harsh green carpet;

This is their habit, the three of them, these winter mornings.

And this is my time for being with him afterwards. When I hear
    the others go downstairs I come to him,

Finding him spread squarely across a sofa, shirt and tie and brown
    suit pulled straight on again over his sweat.

He needs me there. Alone, he might drop the bottle and be upset;
    he might go down to thresh on the carpet again. I
    think this could happen.

But now he's still, only his fingers working through his stubble
    hair, suddenly across the face, down the bent nose:

The colours in his eyes have run together, and he stares up at the
　　　unlit bulb that keeps constant distance from him as he
　　　floats backwards to the ice.

He says nothing, though his mouth is open. Whisky is a fluid
　　　squeezed out of damp ropes, wrung out of short sweaty
　　　hair.

He's glad to have me just sitting.

She has left an empty glass, a cigarette butt in the fireplace and a
　　　tissue here in the wastebasket;

The man an empty glass and the present of a cigar for him to
　　　smoke after lunch, when the television sports shows start.

Those two always choose the morning: a time when he's barely
　　　civil.

The carpet straightens its pressed patches. Drifting back where he
　　　sits he travels it like a cloud shadow, breathing more
　　　gently.

The bull's eye in its jar of formalin, usually on the mantelpiece,
　　　still sits out of harm's way on the cupboard-top.

6 *The Foyer*

The foyer's revolving doors are fixed open to let the dull heat
　　　come and go;
This afternoon, old woman, the hotel extends a long way through
　　　the streets outside: further than you've just been, further
　　　than you can get.

Collapsed long-legged on a public armchair beside the doorway
　　　under the lamp whose straight petals of orange glass hide
　　　its bulbs,
You can't see the indoor buildings along the street;

You can see only me, roofed in with lassitude in the armchair
        opposite,
Against the brown panelling, under the criss-crossed baize letter
        board.

And not even that do you see, one hand spread like a handkerchief
        over the middle of your face –
My hand feels cautiously across my summer haircut; my suit's too
        big.

Your dress and cardigan, flowery and crisp, stand away from your
        brown collapse and resignation like a borrowed hospital
        bathrobe.

The heat flushes you in patches, the confinement takes your breath;

So many things are ochre and mahogany: the days, the flowers,
        an attempt to look a dog in the eye;

This seems to be the place where they wrap us in paper and tie
        us with string.

Though the windows are square and dingy here they're too big
        for you, the ceilings too high to think about,

The doorway too lofty.

To cut any sort of figure going out, you'd have to let me carry you
        through on my shoulders.

7 *The Wrong Time*

It's the wrong time; that makes it the wrong room:
I'm here, he's not; he was here, he will be.

Meanwhile, please use the place. It can use you,
Your scent, silk, clean lines, mouthwash conversation.
With him away it's sour and frowsty. You have
To swell your light to absorb the faint bulb, scuffed greenish walls,
        breakfast wreckage,
Till the silk stitches hurt. You win. But the place contains me.

I'm not what you want. You're not what I want. What do you do
      with me?
Do you take me in, with the milk in the bottom of the bottle;
      dazzle me, with the grease spots, out of reckoning?

Or do you see round me, a man-shaped hole in the world?

Looking at you, I can't tell. You don't seem to find it hard,
      either way.

8 *Truants*

That huge stale smile you give –
Was it ever fresh?

Ancient sunlit afternoon
On a ground floor below street level.
The back window,
Curtained with dark chenille,
        spinach-coloured,
Gives on to a brick wall.

Poor quarters for you, old carcass,
But the cushions are fat over the springs;

You had plenty in that bottle, too.

For me, this is a truancy,
Five minutes' tram ride out of town
In the wrong direction:
I could feel trapped.

      You're different,
Truant entirely, inside your smile.

Two grown-up people.

9 *The Arrival*

You have entered, you have turned and closed the door, you have
    laid down a package wrapped in cloth as dull as your
    clothes and skin.

You have not looked at me, you have not looked for me, you have
    not expected me.

You busy yourself with the package, bending over it, your scuffed
    backside towards me.

You remain in the dirty shadow that edges the room, filtered
    through the fringed green lampshade; only here, just in
    front of me, does the light fall on the carpet.

You would think the light had eaten it away down to the threads.

You, being you, would expect the light to do a thing like that.

You wouldn't notice.

You might expect the faint smell of gas in here to have materialised
    into something like me. I want to go out.

You might notice my leaving. I shouldn't like that.

10 *The Billiard Table*

Morning. Eleven. The billiard table has been slept on.
A mess of sheets on the green baize.
Suggests a surgery without blood.

Starting the day shakily, you keep glancing at it
Till the tangle looks like abandoned grave-clothes.

And watching it from where I sit
I see it's the actual corpse, the patient dead under the anaesthetic,
A third party playing gooseberry, a pure stooge, the ghost of a
    paper bag;

Something that stopped in the night.

Have you ever felt
We've just been issued with each other
Like regulation lockers
And left to get on with it?

Nobody would expect
We'd fetch up in a place like this,
Making unscheduled things like what's on the table.

No longer part of us, it's still ours.

Bring the milk jug, and let's christen it.

THE SHIP'S ORCHESTRA

(1966)

The Ship's Orchestra

The Ivory Corner was only a wooden section of wall painted white, at the intersection of two passageways. To the left of it was the longer corridor; to the right at once there was the washroom door.

Ivory Corner for leaning against, the white pressing the forehead, the wood's vertical grain flickering beneath it up and down across the horizontals of the eyelids.

Washroom door swings, has weight, has rubber silencers. Limbs overhanging it from the Ivory Corner get foggy, the elbow gone, winging; a hand spread on the panel beside it stays brown and dry and shiny.

Always the chance of meeting that walking white suit with a big orange on it for a head; the white yellowed a little, as if through some sort of commerce with urine.

Then it was her black (purple, juice) net dress, rough to the touch, things grew so big in the dark. Or lacquered hair, dry and crisp as grey grass. Want it to come away in handfuls, and she be meek, and satisfied, as far as that. Plimsolls, the smell of feet in a boy's gymnasium. Learn to live with it.

Merrett calls his saxophone a tusk. What shape is the field of vision the eyes experience? Its edges cannot be perceived. A pear-shape, filled with the white plastic tusk, rimmed and ringed and keyed with snarly glitters, floating importantly. Where? Against a high, metallic and misty sunset, the sky like Canada in thaw, and Billy Budd's feet dangling out of heaven five miles up, through a long purplish cloud.

Potential fracture of Merrett's saxophone: by stamping, quick treading, sudden intemperate swing against an upright. In section rather like the break in a piece of dry coconut. No, it would not be likely to bleed. Just the steward brushing up bits of powdered saxophone from the saloon carpet, and Merrett, if surviving, looking out to sea.

Behind the rubber-stopped door, the birth-basins.

Then it was her back, so broad and curved and deeply cleft, doughy and dry to the touch, like some porous cushioning that could not feel. The desiccated hair, yes, distinctly loose; all my senses precarious. I thought of the sheets as black, all hard things there are as ebonite, the indulgent back as very faintly luminous where I touched it; yet I was aware of something brusque in the air: a scented bonfire.

At times the sea rises uniformly to become much of the sky, harmless, translucent, golden-grey, with the great sun billowing down under the keel and flaking off itself from ear to ear. A wake of hundreds of scooped-out grapefruit halves.

Amy, too, in some of her moods, calls her trombone an axe. And the piano, whether I play it or not, is one of the kinds of box. Tusk, axe, box together joined. White baby grand box in scalloped alcove.

Janus, old door-god, your front face is alabaster, fringed with tooled curls, your cheeks and frontal prominences agleam; but a petrified, pitted arse, rained on for centuries, is all that confronts what's on the other side.

Dougal never actually speaks of his bass, even. But Joyce, the girl on drums, doesn't know too much yet. Judge the moment right and we can get her to call them anything. Tubs. Cans. Bins. Bubs.

A waterfall of orange-coloured deckchair canvas, from top to bottom as far as I can see either way without moving my eyes. And a long scroll – I can see the bottom of that, it is weighted with a short pole – covered with dimly printed instructions and transit data. Between these two, the projecting angle of two white-tiled walls at intersection. A narcissistic young passenger – I did not notice of which sex – has just left the picture, dressed for sunbathing.

Consideration of a porthole. Not punched or cut, but made by enormous controlled suction of plane surface away from chosen point of orifice; to be banded, clamped, bolted, glazed. For Merrett to regard the sea, his head resting as if provisionally on his small Napoleonic shoulders. Dougal has spoken to each of us in turn, to say 'Four days at sea, and they haven't asked us to play.' I believe he has also written these same words in a diary, the only entry so far. Dougal concerns himself a great deal with this question of our status, and Amy at least is beginning to be suspicious about his musicianship. This may be because, however obscurely, Amy is American, and is plainly a negress; being black, stringy and big-mouthed, although she wears her hair straight, while Dougal is equally plainly a late British Empire seaport (Liverpool) Spade; tall and medium brown, with quiet eyes and cropped ginger hair and a neat moustache of the same colour. There isn't a leader in fact; we're just a Foster Harris orchestra and if the ship people get any trouble they just wire the office behind your back. But Dougal has to bother.

The white suit with the citrus head ambles by, negotiates the steps with care. It seems benign today.

The taste of the first mouthful of whisky is a thing that creaks, like straining wood, but doesn't quite split.

About five of us, then, and something of an assortment. The coloration problem touches Merrett and me more lightly, in that we are, fairly decidedly, Caucasian, although I can tell already that there's a need for one of us to feel Jewish at times, and we pass this rôle back and forth tacitly. I am sallow and fleshy, with something of a nose, while he is more ruddy, with black hair and a pout. Both of us come from nondescript families; both of us are called Green. He is a Londoner. Both of us are circumcised, too; but so, as it happens, is Dougal. The other oddity is this Joyce, from Nottingham, who looks very young. She must be about seventeen, but doesn't look it: little face, rather pasty (has been sick, though); long blonde hair she can't quite manage; longish nose and big (relatively) dark eyes. Round-shouldered; sometimes a bit damp-looking under the arms. She hasn't unpacked her kit yet. Cans. Bins. Bubs. All five of us double violin.

Think of what all the people you see taste like and you'd go mad: all those leaping, billowing tastes through the world, like a cemetery turned suddenly into damp bedsheets with the wind under them. So the possible taste of a person is a small thing, just a flicker of salt, putrescence, potatoes, old cardboard across the mind, behind the words, behind the manners. And the actual taste, if you go after it, is something that's always retreating; even if it overwhelms, there's an enormous stretch of meaninglessness in it, like the smell of the anaesthetist's rubber mask in the first moments – it ought to mean, it ought to mean; but how can anything mean *that*? There must be a taste about me that could be sensed by others. Somebody as skilled as a dog could recognise it as mine; yet I cannot. If I try to get it from myself I just get the double feeling of tasting and being tasted all in one, like being in a room with an important wall missing. Hold hands with myself as with another person; the hands disappear from my jurisdiction. Looking down, I see moving effigies; the hands that feel are some way off, invisible. There is an image of me that I can never know, held in common by certain dogs.

White wall goes up to a white iron ceiling with big rivets. Windows higher up for a bent gaze. A grey canvas sky with the smoke streaking back from the funnel. This is like those afternoons on shore when everything seems to exist for the window panes. Somebody drumming on the grey canvas roof in my head.

Furniture all over the bandstand and the dance-floor still. The captain was soothing to Dougal, said, 'I can read music very fluently myself, you know.' If you gutted this little white piano here, sealed it and caulked it, it might float.

Joyce's hair by her ears and jutting over her forehead; her nose; the slightly separate gazes of her eyes: something clawlike in all these, latent and neglected. She and the others have been talking and I heard her say she was good at gym at school. Plimsolls, steamed windows; rhythm brushes in the desk.

It splits my head! The great green-glass snout of the sea, the liquid thruster, like an enormous greengage sweet, with bubbles of air in it and the trails of sharks. Presses down into me, through my skull into the back of my nose and throat; peppermint, novocaine, cold and numb. The sky, chalk-blue, squats over it, shaking, pushing. How did I come to be so far down, how did I come to be beneath the ship, to be like a figurehead embedded in the keel? In the flesh of the whole of my right side, from scalp to ankle, there is growing a wet chain, caked with rust. It's not painful; but when I move I can feel my flesh shifting minutely against it. Its tension is different from the tension of my flesh. The old schoolmistress sits at her high desk in the chair with its own footrest. Beside her is a big extension loudspeaker with sunset rays across it in fretwork. Piano music comes from it, and the beating of a tambourine. The old schoolmistress sings, swaying in her chair. The lights are on in the classroom. The little boy lies on the floorboards.

A person is a white damp thing – and here's Amy, who's black and dry – a white damp thing, greyish in some lights even when alive. You could inject salt water into the human body. An all-over emetic. Ha ha. Seminarist. Plankton. Bathyscape. Handkerchief.

Impossible to believe the sound in a piano is so far from the pianist's fingers. I know the keys are ivory boxes filled with wood. In the key of E they seem filled with the pulp of teeth; in G with butterscotch. When I play alone the music is never without a voice or a body.

Lizards, we are all lizards, or will be: khaki-green rubbery lizards prancing agape on a plinth covered with plastic sheeting, over which the cold water is kept running, out of respect for our nature. And we shall not feel sorry for one another when the blunt scissors jag at us and the cold fluids trickle sluggishly out.

Old man up on the boat deck in the morning sun. Sheltered from the wind, wrapped into his chair with a rug. Flattish hat, with the crumpled brim turned up; muffler, sunglasses. Little old man with a clean brown monkey face, mouth like a sloppy purse, liver-coloured lips; hands spread out, spatulate, fingers pressing into the rug. He said to me: 'You are a pianist. I am a masochist.' Merret came up and said, 'Old man, we are going to pick you up by the kneecaps and throw you overboard while nobody is looking.' 'Gentlemen,' he said, 'I am not a homosexual; you misunderstand me.' Etc.

Is it good to feel, under the skin of the chicken as you hold it from running for a moment, the muscles you are going to eat? Oh, questions, questions. How can you crucify a man with a giant orange for a head? The orange falls off once the body slumps down between the strained arms. The shirt collar feebly tries to mouth the last words; you replace the orange, it falls again. You can't put a nail through the orange to hold it to the cross; that's another story. Stand holding it up all afternoon, and the shamefulness of the detachment in the dusk, when he's cold.

A huge yellow oil-drum afloat in the waters of the bay. Sunlight.

Throbber, she said, you're my throbber. And you're my gummy, was the reply. My gummy; my guggy gummy. Now you're my thrubber, she said.

I have known this all along.

Astringency, the prickling of the scalp, flexing of the feet, rotation of the wrists, passing the hands round the confining surfaces of the room where one is. That done, the thought of the scalloped alcove where the band might play. Combed plaster in swirls of rough relief, a deep pink rising from the floor to meet the powdering of gold that thickens and conquers at the zenith. Floor projection forwards, a curved apron, no higher than a tight skirt can step up from maple to black linoleum pitted with marks of casters, drum-spurs, bass-spikes.

Swung from the arms of the gaslamp that was the only light in the street; a street greenish black, among factories. The long linen sack was twisted round and round and was unknotting itself in slow revolutions, with all the weight at the bottom. As it turned, the moisture caught the light, coming through the fabric from top to bottom, but not dripping. Kick.

I am in a poster. This is how the whole thing's meant to appear, obviously. Somebody has been at work on my perceptions, cutting them as giant rudimentary forms out of very thick softboard with a fretsaw, and painting each one a single colour. Although they're only two-dimensional shapes they're thick enough to stand squarely. The ship's superstructure, away over me here in the sunlight, is huge and straight, and of an immensely comfortable white. It's not at all complicated. People, the sky, the sea. The cataract of orange deckchair canvas, the scroll; these are present, and a march of relief-built letters you would need a ladder to climb. An E, an A, a T. You don't have to go and eat. This *is* Eat. Scaffolded, boarded, painted. This is the provision, this is the activity itself. Maybe I have hands a yard wide, a smile like an excavator, nothing matters. The dimensions of the components are not determined by the component subject. Fine. The directors of the shipping line, Foster Harris, the captain of a distillery can be seen queueing by the ballroom door to take credit for this ordering of things. They are small and neatly photographed against the placid outsize expressionism of this set. Then there's the sun. This is Eat. It says it is, so it is. Things seem what they are, believe it.

Looking at this world that is like cake, this fifth day at sea, I realise that Amy, Merrett, Joyce and Dougal are probably happy people, to whom a day like this is nothing strange. And I was thinking of them lying down below on their straw, sniffing and shifting about. Joyce on her straw. Merrett on his straw. Joyce with her clothes too thin to ward off prickling, Merrett with nowhere to put his glasses and his trousers too tight to lie down in comfortably. Dougal on his straw, lying on his thin shoulders and knobbly buttocks, scratching, scratching, his long fingers always squeezing at his skin. Amy on her straw, hard and glossy, waiting for her belt, her dress, her skin itself to split under the strain of not caring. In fact I know Dougal and Joyce are playing draughts, Amy reading magazines, and Merrett lying benign on his bunk playing cat and mouse with a hangover. Snug little figures in the big poster. We are getting to be like the passengers. They should let us play, perhaps; treat us in some little way as if we were a band of musicians. Little way, big way: the dimensions of the components are not determined by the component subject. It doesn't matter. I see, coming up a stair, through a door, round a corner, up an open companionway across a deck, through a door and out of sight, going, the actor who must be going to take the part of me in the immortalisation of these days – their 'rendering'. Bigger than I would have expected, and a bit old-world. Tuxedo, black hair, suntan, highpowered eyebrows, searching brown eyes; boyish manner preserved in maturely male bulk (shruggable shoulders, big back). Glasses in breast pocket, presumably. Do Merrett, Dougal, Joyce, Amy, see their actors and actresses today? Probably not. Why did I have to see mine? I didn't want to spoil the poster by appearing as myself. Why not? This is Eat. Take what comes.

Throwing up in the washroom the other day I had a vision of a dark pink, double-tailed mermaid. I haven't been seasick this trip, so far as I know: this was the little drunk I went on with Merrett and Amy to get settled in. There's a binary phase in this kind of vomiting, especially marked if your balance is fairly good. A strong consciousness of two ears, two shoulders, two knees, feet, elbows, sets of fingers gripping the edges of the basin; these two sets of characteristics existing each on its side of the room. Between them is a void, a gully; and that is the vomiting. It was in a sort of clear sky above this gully that I saw the mermaid; just at the moment when the idea of being sick rises to the ears, brims and fills them like a sea, the sight goes and the sudden assault on the pharynx arrives, and the invasion of the facial expression. She was floating Botticelli-fashion against a green-ish watery sky and some way up from some very stylised olive-green waves. The two tails, in obvious concession to the binary thing, pointed to left and right, and were, at the extremities at least, green as the waves. For the rest, apart from some rather nondescript-coloured hair, she was coloured this remarkable deep pink, uniformly, without variation of tone: lips, nipples, finger nails, the one eye she had open, everything. It was the pink of scouring paste or a rather sickly tulip, a little bluish, yet very bold. Although clearly breathing, and even moving a little, she looked like a figure in a primitive painting whose artist, while realising that flesh wasn't white, hadn't got down to details. She was a burly girl, with fat rubbery cheeks and round arms; looking out of her left eye at me as though she had never seen anything like me before.

Amy has begun to play: the first of us. I can hear it through the wall. She has got out her trombone case, removed the instrument, and is blowing it. Long notes, staccato series. Methodical, clear, accurate; says nothing. Amy is a killer, a musical shark. For those who want that kind of treatment. She'll not bother with me. She must be feeling low, to have to play.

Soon there will be a meal. The food will pity me, I shall pity myself. Healthy, ambulant, I am about to be fed with cosy food that tries to make up for my being far from home, my being a great big boy criminal. The seat will be soft, the things clean, my last mess mopped and laundered. And until that big soothing spreads towards me the little notes of the trombone hammer away, like brass shell-cases on a moving belt. It is the sort of time when something very large and wide and silvery, like the capsized hull of a vast ship, can begin slowly to rise above the horizon.

Reasons. The ship is a unity. Enclosed within its skin of white paint it floats upon, and chugs across, the unified ocean. Some would think of it as having the shape of cleavage, a narrow leaf: to me it is a flat canister bearing another canister and a similarly cylindrical funnel, the basic canister shape being eccentrically elongated. This is because the vessel's speed is not great and, whereas there are those who would see the superstructure as a vague and mutable spectre above the hull, it is that hull that appears ghostly to me, while the funnel never altogether leaves my thoughts. At any rate the ship is a unity and does one thing: it proceeds on its cruise. Not only does it have a structural and purposive unity; it has a music which proceeds with it, sounds within it and makes signals of the good life. In among the musicians is the tough glass bubble of the music. Reasoning, now. The musicians don't play. No bubble. The ship is not a unity. It is not white. It is grey, indigo, brown. Thin girderworks of green, and orange even, and coils of pale yellow piping. It is not a series of canisters; it is a random assembly of buildings which, though important-looking, have no proper streets between them. It does not float; its parts are arrested in their various risings and fallings to and from infinite heights and depths by my need for them to be so. The funnel cannot be said to crown the firm structure; rather it juts rakishly over inconsequential forms and looks when the sky is dirty like the chimney of a crematorium suspended above the waves. The ship does not proceed on its cruise, but opens and closes itself while remaining in one spot. The ocean is not a unity but a great series of shops turned over on to their backs so that their windows point at the sky.

O captain. Is it the captain? O first officer? Is it the first officer? Etc.

Such heavy straps and buckles for so young a girl to wear! Such a stiff casing and mask, such mechanical magnification of the voice to stridency! Such a channelled street, with iron pavements for her to strut down, so young!

Monitors, those curious warships there used to be. Little vessels that each carried one enormous gun. Restless home lives of their captains.

The rings of winter, the circles of winter. Why? The hoops and bands of frost. Cooperage that fetches the skin off. Why circles when it goes cold? There are times when you can live as if in a round pond, keeping on moving even when it freezes. And overlapping ponds all round, across the gardens and the streets; making up the sea when the land stops. The rings are there but nobody can ever see them.

Think of Joyce's mother. An accordioniste, maybe, toothy, gilded somewhere, and with a hollow at her throat you could rest your nose in after a hard day's work. To turn her child into this, what can she be? Yet the girl thinks of herself as a jazz musician; talks about Blakey and Roach, or mentions them when pressed. Think of Amy's mother. Difficult. Think of Merrett's mother; of Dougal's mother. Of mine.

He was in a garden all walled about and set amid the sea. And he came into a place where there was a soft-faced flower like a cup on a single stem; the bloom a little larger than his own head and its top a handsbreadth taller than he. And soon the flower lay down on a low bed that was in the place and gave him to understand he should lie on the bed beside it. And he did so. Whereat the flower lay close with him and softly folded him in its leaves, as well as it was able. And he was aware of a marvellous scent from the flower, and would have swooned, etc. And forthwith the flower made great to do to unloose the fastenings of his garments, even to the buttons of his braces. And right hard the work proved, whereas the flower had not fingers but the points of its leaves only. So in this wise passed a longer while than that of all that went before.

The rings of summer for that matter. Carry on.

This is what it is like on the land. She: she holds court facing up-stream, on a handrailed plank bridge over the yellow floodwater of a ditch cut into the clay to hold a gas main. The gas and the clay stink like dung in the cold; pink smoke jets from a vent high in an isolated building some way off. The place is surrounded by white canvas screens, damp and grubby. Over her waved dark red hair is spread a muslin dishcover with a bead fringe. Angry brown eyes, pasty skin in folds down to the dewlaps and scrawny neck. Head raised, wide mouth pulled into disapproval. She sits straight-backed in the old cane armchair, propping herself on one elbow. One leg is crossed over the other and the fluffy slipper points ele-gantly. Apart from the slippers, the dishcover and a pair of baggy pink drawers, she wears nothing.

Merrett, Dougal, it is you and I who have put her there; struggling in our leather breeches through the mud of the site, carrying her at shoulder height in the cane chair; Joyce, Amy, in dungarees and waders you were there too. We must be together in some-thing. Far off across the wet land there are conical fires perhaps and men turned into meat.

The rings of summer would be visible if they existed. The powder we used to make orangeade from, cast in big circles on the ocean, and the circles widening and fading as the powder sinks, in cur-tains through the depths. And in the empty middles of the circles white things could rise, and float, and disappear. Whalebone spars, cakes of soap, plastic saxophones, tennis shoes.

I saw it from above at dusk as I looked over the rail. On the deck below, it sat hunched, the white suit full of blurred shadows. The head is larger, puffier, more yellowed and sad, and it shows indent-ations which have not filled out again and which seem to be the product not of blows but of violent fondling. I think the end will come, probably by further violence, during the night, or tomorrow at the latest.

My head. The huge shimmering cloud-filled canister that supports it by describing its furthest limits is shaking irregularly in the night breeze. There is light on the waves, and the ship is a dark factory.

Ivory Corner, white and shining phosphorescent, a tongue that licks me slowly as I approach, from toes to scalp, and extinguishes it-self at my back.

I have talked to many people today. I have talked a great deal. The question of our not being asked to play has gone cold, even among ourselves. We are accepted everywhere as what we have become. People go off to bed early in the silence. The absence of music is somebody's urbane whim, and they respect it. Maybe there is somebody slow who will notice, tomorrow or the next day, and be indignant, just as Dougal was at first. But think now of those dozens of silent black aridities moving about the ship, going into cabins, losing momentum, sleeping, turned inside out in the dark like rubber gloves.

There's a labyrinthine system, running all through the ship, of whatever it is that rules by default the minds of the incurious. Slippery wet blackness, invisible by day. Sacs, coiled tubes of it, linking all the people, deck to deck, dream to dream.

I once actually met one of those men who say to you, 'As a matter of fact, sexual thoughts and activities play a very small part in my life.'

Pink smoke jets from a vent high in the wall. Ibis-coloured. In the yellow ditch float bottles of clear glass.

At sunset Merrett grew frightened and stopped drinking. He tried to tell Dougal and me stories about himself. We listened quietly, for I had not been drinking and the stuff seems to have no effect on Dougal. Merrett, in the red sunbeams, talked and laughed with us, while the coming of night alarmed him.

Then it was her black net dress, rough to the touch, and the warm dry scent everywhere catching the breath; and it was the grey desiccated hair floating and filling the room, the dress and the hair up to the ceiling, the room a skirt, the hair in the ceiling corners with the smoke; hair from her scalp, legs, belly. Useless to open my eyes, I was blinded with touch. But her skin was nowhere; the body was away. She had filled the room with her dress and the dead hair. Pouflam! The fire caught it.

She is among the hollyhocks, she is on hands and knees among the rhubarb, she is legging it over the low fence in the dusk. She still has the black dress. She still has the grey hair. I see it behind the petrol pump where she is standing, her back to it, pretending to hide. She is too mad. She doesn't really feel what happens to her. I insist that she must. Who made her mad? If she were really to go bald her breasts would become beautiful, etc. I have to be sentimental about her, for her own safety.

I wake, and ebony poles are across me from wall to wall, a few inches above my face. No farther apart than the bars of a baby's cot. There's a grey dawn light travelling the cabin; it goes. No. Sleep again, in this paper leaf. I have wet myself, I have died. No. In my sleep they have anaesthetised me and with their toothless rubber jaws they have gnawed away my genitals entirely. Cleaned me up – I hear one of them still mumbling it. I dare not touch yet. The grey light, the white light, the dull disc of waking. Not yet. In the night Amy comes to me now. She strips her hard black body, a piece of furniture, and presses it down on me where I lie as if she would break my bones. And with the expanding mandibles that have replaced my privates I clasp her and contain her sadism for hours without motion, until she lifts herself off, quietened, though still taut. Her straightened hair sticks up in a crest as she digs her fingers through it. She fastens her white towelling robe and gives me a dog's snarl of a smile as she goes.

Amy does not come to me in the night.

My actor goes past, treading lightly, his big shoulders affable. He greets me; I respond. He has useless-looking hands of course. Who will play for the soundtrack, will there be any soundtrack, etc. As well as his own breakfast, he has eaten mine.

Visceral pipes of white porcelain, huge things, in banks and coils, too wide to straddle. How to get lost in the morning. They reach up in stubby loops and descend far beneath, the systems crossing, curving round, running in parallel. Some plunge vertically through several levels then divide and disappear; some come creeping through the interstices of others as if squeezed before cooling. At the top, the light strikes hard and bright, softening and blurring at the next levels.

Deep down there is only the little light that drips deviously through the chinks. Every so often there is an open end, pointing upwards.

Potential fracture of the pipes.

Hope-pipes, love-pipes, fright-pipes, thought-pipes, loss-pipes, hate-pipes. Pipes of coarseness, pipes of sanity. Pipes of confession. Pipes of purity, pipes of sanctity, pipes of flight. Riding-pipes, rubbing-pipes, sliding pipes, wiping-pipes, confronting-pipes, adoring-pipes.

Potential fracture of the pipes. Virtually impossible. Only single-handed with a light sledgehammer, squatting on the topmost U-bend and clouting at the pipe until it cracks and shows the ochre stuff it's made of. Then bashing at the necks down to the levels, smashing across the fat conduits that curve down, caving in long sections of horizontal pipe from above, then standing in the channels and striking out at the sides till the brittle catwalk underfoot collapses; the débris all the while shuffling its way down in shards and dust into the open mouths and between the pipes to the bottom of the whole system. Descending, the need for clearing the rubbish from the pipes to get a foothold; the monotony of the straight stretches; the strength of the main joints. Arrival at the level where the débris no longer shifts, but has accumulated to this height up from the floor; and how far down that is, under rubbish and unbroken pipes, it is impossible to discover except by reaching down to it. Then the task is to probe for the buried pipes, shattering them among the surrounding fragments, never being able to clear their surfaces any more, but hammering at them blind through what covers them. The excavation of hollows to work in; the seepage back of the broken pieces down the slopes. The laceration of the boots and gloves, the sensation of the feet sinking deeply into the jagged shale; the pipeless walls of the system's container staring inwards at one another, feeling the new light down themselves towards what is at the bottom.

Then it was that man learned to fly. Unfolded from the middle of his waistband by the pulling outwards of a black cord was the creased brown paper bird-form, crackling in the sunshine and peeling itself out bigger across his belly and chest, pushing his shoulders back and flap-wrapping around them. The tail that flattened itself across his thighs; the paper membrane that stopped his nose and mouth, closed his eyes and clapped wind at his ears in immense distance. The railway that ran southward across the smooth ugly sea.

Dropping from the sky and going fast, a cone of paper or some composition fibre, white tipped with red. Disappears below my lower lids, behind whatever is there for it to disappear behind. Effusion of aeronaut; part of a trombone mute; spiritual part of man-made cat.

The paper membrane that stopped his nose and mouth, closed his eyes and clapped wind at his ears in immense distance. The hand that at the same moment walked its long fingers up the back of his neck and through his hair, prodding quite hard, treating his head as something unlikely to burst, letting the pointed nails pivot in the skin as the fingertips turned over. Joyce.

Joyce, who looks at people sometimes as if she lived in their bodies and had just moved a few feet away to get a better look. When her life invades her daze. Too soon yet for anybody to tell her.

Her looks, not her life, invading the daze. The life's not powerful enough to alter without the looks. But in that pasty little face the mouth is going to be wide, with an upper lip that pulls back at the corner. The brows will be thick over the irregular eyes and the nose long and straight, with a knobbly end. Some of her postures foreshadow these changes.

The mouth. Fills the area of vision, is very close. Soft, the woman's mouth, impossible to tell whose. Colours fade towards vapour. Closer, there is nothing but the lips, their joining line rising and falling along their shapes, the wrinkling in of the surfaces towards the line. Slowly the line retreats, the lips part, widen; the teeth can be seen, the gentle tongue, not quite motionless, the spaces of the mouth, capable of holding a clear note of music. The breath must taste of cold water. From the right Merrett walks on, the lower lip level with his knee. Seeing the open mouth, he peers forward; then, putting his hands into his jacket pockets, steps carefully over the lower teeth and into the mouth, ducking his head. He walks cautiously about, looking up, down and around; but does not go anywhere out of sight. He ducks again under the top teeth, steps carefully over the lower, and comes out. Then he goes on his way. The mouth stays open.

Somewhere there's going to be some music. I haven't the courage myself to clamber over what keeps me from the piano, to plunge my fingers into its clashes of sound. And what I play isn't what I mean by music. Breath music. Slow opaque music. The ship has come close, drawn itself up my body and continues to rise. Yet it is, though fitted to me, nevertheless very big and stretches far away from me above and below and on all sides. And all the compartments of which it is made are full of milky sounds ready to knock against the bulkheads and echo all through the vessel.

The captain's hat revolves, returns, revolves, returns, never completing a revolution. The captain breakfasts above the clouds, on thoughts invented for him by Dougal.

Great glycerine drops of water trickled down the girl's bedraggled hair, were caught in her eyebrows, ran down her nose and off its tip. Down her checks and neck, cascades. All over her chilled lumpish flesh, the big grey eyes looking down at it, the wide mouth curving,

56

the tongue licking the drip in from its corner. A rivulet between the breasts, spreading across the steep belly. Twisted streams down each breast and falling from the cold plug-nipples. Water standing in separate shiny drops on her big thighs.

Corridor of grey mucus. A kidney bowl of it behind each door.

Over the white linoleum floor the nurse advances with the orange gladioli arranged in a spray, then goes off behind whatever she goes behind. A tap forcefully turned on. The nurse is mature, ladylike, and of fair complexion.

Dougal tranquil, nodding down there in a canvas chair, his cuffs rolled back, the gilt strap of his wristwatch gleaming. His cigarette, cocked between his fingers, burns down. Then which of us is worried?

Shirt cuffs folded back, right above the elbow, whites of eyes showing. Let's go to church to see the dog given its fix.

Merrett said last night that his alto would dent rather than fracture; and that he also had in his trunk an ordinary plated metal tenor, not so handsome, but capable, he said, of cracking a man's skull if you hit him hard enough with it.

Blue fog. Electric cigars. E-flat horns wired in series. *Camions*. One eye at a time, one eyebrow at a time. Dougal dozes. For Dougal to have his proper beauty the circumstances of his life – waking, going to sleep, washing, eating, defecation, micturition – need to be regarded as clinical conditions, their operations supervised by trained nurses.

The two little scrubbers hugging each other in Merrett's bed in the hotel, both of them snivelling and complaining; and Merrett, in shirt and trousers, lying rigidly under the covers on the edge of the bed. Scene from Merrett's first professional job, as clarinettist in a traditional band touring out of London. The bed, Merrett's and the banjo-player's; the idea, the banjo-player's. Nocturnal disappearance of the banjo-player.

All this disposal business, these basins, enamel buckets, plunging tubes, embalming sluices, constant jets, sterile bins, sealed incinerators, consideration of where the banjo-player might have gone that night, of the abolition of words taped to our memories, of the storage of one night under another night, the earlier ones gradually fading as the multi-track builds up beyond the bounds of desire;

all this question of the attenuation of substance to concepts. Are there in the ship's mortuary yellow-soled feet with the toes sticking up and facial lines of resignation showing on them in their stillness? Where are our instruments? They luggage us, they follow us, they squat behind us when we're not looking. The facts are these. Merrett's plastic alto in case beneath port-hole. His tenor locked away in his trunk. Dougal's bass, in cover, standing behind the door of the small room behind the bandstand. Joyce's drums, boxed and cased, in the same place. In Dougal's cabin, two violins in fabric cases edged with leatherette and an acoustic guitar in a polythene bag. In Amy's, the polished trombone, with chasing all round the bell, its mouthpiece set against Amy's lips, while she blows long notes, very quietly. In the corner, a small guitar and amplifier. In my cabin a stack of folders of standard invertible reversible orchestrations, song copies and manuscript paper. The white baby grand piano, locked, its lid down with crates of tonic bottles stacked on it, in the scalloped pink and gold alcove. Disposal.

Potential utter disposal of the instruments, itemised disposal (as stamping on the violins, hammering the drums flat-sided, sawing the piano into slices like a ham, turning the trombone into an artificial flower, fighting a duel with the guitars, shredding the bass with pliers and chisel) being too crude and guilty. An engine is necessary: a hangar stretching some miles in all directions, with every part of it, outside and in, painted matt white. Semi-opaque panels to admit much diffused light. The instruments fitted into white foam rubber containers sealed laterally and set in further containers sealed longitudinally, these last being cylindrical and of uniform size, about ten feet in both length and diameter. As many as possible of these cylinders; all must be uniformly weighted, and each must have an identifying number stencilled on it consisting of a number of digits equal to the total number of cylinders, only one digit on each cylinder varying from the norm established in the first numeral, and the varying digit not to be in the same position in the sequence on any two cylinders. Filling the hangar, a continuous white tube into which the cylinders fit and in which they are moved pneumatically at a steady speed. Further details of solvent tanks, sludge filtering and caking, moulding of cake into casing of fissile explosive device, recording of distribution of post-explosive material, public opinion poll, suspension of communications for necessary periods, change of languages, etc.

Without the instruments: we can all share a taxi and spend the afternoon at somebody's sister's wedding party. Wellington boots, exuberance, ducks and drakes on the park lake with crumby plates.

How the sloping shed of a Saturday evening in England falls over Joyce, over me, over Dougal, Merrett, over sad Amy. We do not play, we are people. Dougal embraces Amy in a delivery van, Merrett and I go to a gymnasium just before it closes. Joyce is one of the little girls who giggle at us as we go in.

This is what it is like on the land: on ground where disused vehicles are dumped, a woman has given birth to a child in a giant aeroplane tyre.

On the land the oil-refineries strain to escape from themselves along the river banks but cannot move, and the sky on its conveyor comes round and round again.

On the land the men swarm over the new concrete obstacles and fill the spade's ravines with their ebullient bodies. Let us build again!

The ship's orchestra is at sea. Crammed into a high and narrow compartment in a heated train on a penal railway, we loom out of the shadows at one another in our full dignity at last, between the brownish light of the windows on either side, light that fails to reach right into the domed ceiling of the compartment. The light paints over Merrett's glasses and covers his eyes. Amy's cheekbones are luminous in the tobacco shadows; our heads reach up close to one another, preternaturally large from narrow shoulders and stretched bodies. We are about to agree.

Perhaps the little white piano has useless dampers, and however good the others are my playing will be a continuity of shining brass water, shaking idiotically. Have the others wondered whether I can play? Pianists who go about alone usually can. For my part I have seen Dougal stowing his bass behind the door; have heard him scat odd bars; I have heard Merrett blow a few sodden flourishes on his alto when he took it out to show it to me as soon as we were drunk; I have not seen Joyce anywhere near her drums, but I have heard her humming to herself. I have heard Amy's short notes, and her long notes; and what appeared to be a series of arpeggios of the chord of the fifteenth, with the fifth, seventh, ninth and thirteenth degrees flattened in various combinations as the afternoon proceeded. Some of them slowed her up a little, but it would have been an achievement even for a woman who was sober. Amy has stayed drunk in order to break Joyce in, it appears.

All the same, we're about to agree. The guards are laying the jumping chains out in the sunlit courtyard. The lizards scuttle for shelter. The weeds that have had links dragged roughly over them straighten up slowly.

The old man on the boat deck, sitting wrapped in his rug, turned his sunglasses towards us and, seeing us all together for once, suggested to Merrett, Dougal and me that we ought to dress as women. It took him some while to make clear what he meant, and when he had finished he sat laughing and laughing, his mouth open all the time. Amy was much amused too, and wouldn't let the idea go. It turns out that she is the only one of us who has actually been married.

The white suit going round the corner into the washroom, shuffling with a stick. The length of the corridor away, and the light bad; but the head appeared to be bandaged.

My body explored slowly by squares of differently coloured light. Odd sensation. The little slanted rectangles alter the sizes of the parts of my body they touch from moment to moment and leave a black creek of me in among themselves, that waves and shakes itself about in pursuit of them. The flapping black unseen part of me: a unity.

A covering of sacking over me, that I needn't move. Beyond it there is a room distempered pale green. Smell of soap. Inside the sack, in here with me I think.

The big standing dog. The silent dog. The chimney is stuffed up, the cracks round the doors and window sealed. The brown dog, motionless, grows to completion within the room. Nothing to consider there but its rough matted coat, its deep flanks.

The porthole of enormous strength has come among us and stands, turning this way and that to be admired. Adversative at all times but turning, turning always to make peace. The big standing porthole. The brown compartment. Our soap-sack, our own, the scent of which guides us back to ourselves in the night. The dog's huge stale smile, its mountainside of coat; the silence of its smile.

Hear the lining of the chaps part here and there from the gums, the saliva and air making sound in there. Sound that peels back behind the bulkheads, across ceilings; up and down the backs of the legs. Sound fitted with a glass eye.

Inside the wet aeroplane tyre: when there are enough strips of bacon rind we shall weave him a little coat.

Sound that moves beneath its clear brown glass, propelled by full sails; that carries reservoirs of ink beneath its waist; that shadows itself as it goes. Sound that swallows pearls into twilight the colour of beer.

Slippery sound, retarded till it fractures into many transparent wedges, then into countless pools of travelling light, within each of which great black streets stretch themselves before the wind-screens of lampless vehicles, travelling fast. Sound that polishes the stinking dust and makes it stand up in the night, before the wardrobe mirrors, while the gloves deflate, crinkling in the dark.

The sound of hundreds of feet of film, split from their reels on to the store cupboard floor, being trampled in the dark by the animal shut in there.

If Merrett, Dougal and I dress as a woman, become women, will Amy and Joyce have to become men?

There'll be no need.

In the domed compartment, so ill-lit, where the spilled celluloid crinkles out of sight under our shoes, Amy's knees touch mine as the train sways; Dougal's knees touch Amy's and mine; Merrett's knees touch Amy's and mine and Dougal's; Amy's, Merrett's, Dougal's and my knees touch Joyce's as the train continues to sway. If only we could all play together on one single instrument!

Ivory Corner for Joyce; on the white paintwork a big lipstick mouth to kiss her. Ivory Corner for Amy: padded hooks, to hold her up by the shoulder-straps.

Ivory Corner for Merrett: with a heavy iron disc to press down on to the crown of his head when he stiffens upward. Ivory Corner for Dougal: Joyce, standing stark naked and freezing cold, with her eyes shut, at two in the morning.

To be somebody else: to be Amy. Like this. The men push me out of the washroom if I go in there. Grabbing my elbows, knee in my butt, hand shoving my head forwards at the door. One pulls the door open and the others shove me against it so that the white edge of it comes between my knees, splits the skirt, strikes up my belly, and my teeth and nose come hard against it. This is to make the black ape-woman swear; the bitch whimper for her fix.

What do they think I want? The sea coming up my street, fast, kicking up my nose, making my calf-eyes roll at the sky, splitting me with an explosion of green glass foam? The rifles laid across me in a heap, where I lie naked, the cold bolts thumbing my rifle-coloured skin? To go around smelling of dead flowers again? I don't know what size of things I want.

Anybody, mummify me. It doesn't matter which of them I am.

The little shrivelled black monkey, growing smaller and smaller. The blue above: morning in Sky Gulf. The monkey's owner knocks nails into a piece of board to make music for it.

And the alabaster kingfisher plummeting upwards through the grey photo-print of the water for minutes on end, out of sight. Dedicated.

She's wet all over, with a thin film of something slightly viscous, almost like very watery cement. It must be dropping from somewhere overhead. Cold sweat out of the metal. Not so much on the hair though. Glistens: phosphorescent, the sheen wavering as she breathes. Her lips are lightly stuck together with the stuff, and the eyelids too.

Why has Joyce been crying?

The single instrument would have to be an inflated ring, like a tyre-tube. When it's wet whatever rubs across it raises a squeal. Each of us to have an undefined territory on the circuit. Not really a tangible thing even though it's our common body; but it's as if there was an invisible sphincter in the sky somewhere, with a fivefold answer to our touches.

Buckle the lamps in close to the ribs, rub salt on to the pale peaks of the shoulders, clasp stones wrapped in rag in each armpit; paint the mouth of the navel with lipstick. Pin newspaper cuffs round the nipples and the groin; whether it is a man or a woman is immaterial, but shave the legs and forearms in any case. Whoever it is will need to stand up throughout. Thin white steampipes run down the pink wall.

I am something that has been pushed out of Amy's body, though I cannot remember it. I have no legs, though I have the idea of legs, and I have no arms or hands, though I can conceive of them;

but I can move my head this way and that, where I lie. She knows I have come out but she doesn't know where I am.

It would upset her very much to learn that I can move my head in this way, and I shall take care that she never finds out. My eyebrows are beautifully thick and curved, incidentally.

A thin brass ring goes bouncing down steps noisily. And still the orchestra is about to agree.

Bandaged, I am something that has been pushed out of Merrett's body in his sleep. Although I can run and jump I have no head at all. I think I am yellow.

What appears to be human hair hangs in long ropes, caked with runs of white sediment, from the gantries the ship must pass under to get to the sky again. Just a few of these ropes of hair, fairly easy to avoid.

There is dangling in the little concrete laboratory, too, from surprised fingers. Twisted black, like monkey limb or hair set in bitumen, stuck to itself and dried, and easy to tear. Blander to taste than anyone would think; its smell of sweet banana spreads everywhere.

Flakes of skin on the gantries, flakes of cellulose adhesive coming off in the evening sun. Flakes of grey paint. That grinning dog that eats everything.

There is hair fringing some of these girders that is soft and fair, and combed out. Eyelash hair that curls in the sunlight and flickers in the wind. Once: a belly rubbed with lemon peel. Somebody's.

Cold in the afternoons, cold in the evenings. There is one eye now, stitched open with wire. Flocks of children fall away when I rub my fingers, and ranks of square houses. How big my fingers are.

What does she think when I rub my tanned fingers down the white doorpost, altering the surface; or across one another? What does she think I am doing? Children with dirty faces, inquisitive mouths hanging open; they are always silent. These fingers I rub are hard, the skin feels dead. What does she think they are?

Trapped somehow, arrested in this doorway, dropped on to one knee, this hand that troubles me resting on the other, thumb and fingers crossing, rubbing. Otherwise peaceful. But arrested here. And I am aware of Amy watching me from very close. She has made herself like a rubber moon. And Dougal; and Joyce behind him. And Merrett squats close to me, looking at me like a friend. They are taller, and everything is narrower, bulkier, softer. As I feel them watching me I become incapable of watching them at all. I wonder what they see when they look at my fingers moving.

The light on the black arms of the big machine shows the edges up hard. The iron arms go down across darkness, into broken light, back through darkness and up again, their edges hard. A sizeable piece of worn-looking white cotton stuff is being passed to and fro inside the machine, but it doesn't get dirty.

The face of the stretched undervest. I am not plagued by it, but I know it is there, and its opposite, and its less obvious variants. What is the opposite of a face?

Now there's this trumpet-player, Henrik, come out of the sickbay at last. He looks at me when I'm down, too, friendly, though I never visited him. Cadaverous, sallow man, with cropped grey hair and big moulting brown eyes that weaken his mouth as they move.

I cannot tell how it is lit. In those moments when suddenly I am trapped or down, and they are looking at me, I am aware of nothing but their compassionate eyes. And when it is gone I cannot imagine how the scene was lit. Not by daylight. Something beyond the doorway and the dark panelling.

Horsehair, the padding of an old chair, pulled out in a flat tangle. Sometimes a man's star stains like a cigarette burn on yellow wood.

Suffering and love in Henrik's eyes. A thinking love. Temptation to make him happy, then outwit him.

What does she think when she knows they are close to me?

There is clear brown glass, there are pink flowers, there is the dark panelling. The distance of late afternoon sun.

A long hand with a tremor rests on the metal arm of a black machine. The thumb rubs drily across the iron, across the side of the forefinger.

A journey. Between Amy's breasts by caterpillar tractor. And back again.

The white porous earth-cloud that passes me through itself, and through; that brings forward more of itself to grow round me, the sounds of factories muffled above my head, beneath my head. To subside through this cloud-bread that puts blind and deaf distance about me.

If she knows they are close to me, she knows she, too, has come close. She sees what Henrik sees when he talks to me.

While Henrik talks to me the others talk to my actor up on deck. With Henrik there is clear brown glass, there are pink flowers, dark panelling. On the land too, there are these things.

A couple of hours before dawn the dry, porous grey fog, webbed with black net. Caked carbon of burnt hair on the lace, sweet smells of the garden at night.

Morning. The actor watching me whenever I go up on deck.

I have been to this convalescent woman's cabin twice already, once in the afternoon, once in the night. She knows I have nothing to do. Her reddish-brown hair is dyed from grey, I think. She's sallow, and rather bony; not exactly elderly, but careful about how she moves, and a little deaf. The first time, the late afternoon sun beat up off the sea through the little curtain; the second time, the faint light from the wall fitting spread out across the panelling without reaching the corners. She watches everything with her brown eyes – doesn't like closing them. In the cabin she says very little. When I'm not with her I don't need to think about her at all. I like a pretty silk frock she has, patterned in grey and red.

The old man on the boat deck no longer says anything as I pass. I go up close and peer at him. Behind the sunglasses his eyes are shut. His hands are folded over his stick, their slight tremors shaking it.

In the swimming pool the actor goes idly along on his back, the sunlit water patterning his breast and belly.

There was a little old man I helped to nurse while he was dying. His paralysed legs grew soft and feminine, his whole body coy. In the coffin he was rouged and decked out in satin frills and ribbons.

The skin of her bared upper arms is pale and flabby, though she is thin. My fingers and my thumbs detect the muscles under the skin. There is a vacancy on her body that her pretty scent does not cover. Across the vacancy her brown eyes follow me.

The water supports the actor, the sun nourishes him, the air delights in his body. The water sprinkles him with stars as he wallows playfully on his back, dipping from side to side.

Suppose she wears nightdresses like the heavy shiny pink one always, not just when I visit. That would be no joke.

The actor's nipples are like the soft oval tops of little puddings flavoured with the palest chocolate, buried in his breast. His flesh absorbs, creamy and riddled with muffled journeys. He is cumulus. The thought of his flesh is a thought rubbed with oranges, painted with honey.

Will she darn the seam we burst open under the arm or will she leave it torn till next time? I know where she keeps her glasses when she takes them off, I can't pretend to myself that I don't. Am I kind to her? Would I be flattered to see the other men she has settled for before me? I think I should not.

The smell of leather passes heavily on the wind to starboard and disappears ahead.

She seems to enjoy me as if she were enjoying something I should not myself like: a shiny, sticky iced cake, for example. That is the newness. If I go many more times she will start to notice me.

Two late afternoons, one after the other. Some repetitions, some variations. Not enough data to set patterns. I play all the time with the simple yes-no toy of whether I go for the second midnight in succession or leave the first to stand as an emergency. Plenty to think about. Nothing gives me a lead.

He flames under the waves in flakes like the setting sun. His navel is an ancient mouth. His teeth strengthen his followers' fingertips as they brush them across his opened lips. His feet, etc. His privy member, handsomely formed, is still as a lizard.

There are circles of beauty across his body. Smiles of beauty across his shoulders. All this has been prepared for: white canvas screens stand about on the deck, flapping tightly in the sun.

Patted dry, he puts on his crisp white jacket again. His fingers, made for smoking cigarettes, settle his collar. He wears his glasses.

Joyce is taller than I thought she was.

Why should they have been doing it in the washroom instead of the sick-bay? Behind the rubber-stoppered door. I had assumed him dead without expecting a funeral. So many other ways. Disposal. But to glimpse the white suit, yellowed, crouched on a stool by the basin while the nurse and the sick-berth attendant were taking the bandages from the head.

The captain has gone down into the depths of the ship; into slippery wet blackness, invisible by day.

I could go to her in the mornings too. Or instead. Perhaps somebody else goes in the mornings. But I was the first, yesterday. She'd had no time after being so ill to get anybody else.

Bent over on to the porcelain it looked at me without any change of expression. Placid, interested in what was happening. Discernibly a human head, bald, with one big eye looking at me. Where the dressing peeled away I could see the contusion, the spontaneous breaks in the skin, the wounds that looked too tired to bleed. All the time he concentrates on his head.

For a moment, a great shaking glass sheet for a window, with the blurred pink figure of a man shouting at me through it. But I cannot hear a sound from him or from the wind that distorts him so.

Dougal comes past. I tell him to avoid the washroom. He thanks me.

She wants to make me forget. That is what she says, starting to notice me. In the darkness, slippery nylon wrinkled against my face, my head full of cold scent, I feel self-pity coming on.

What is it she thinks I can remember? I can never remember enough. Against her side I rub the chain I feel growing in me, but she misunderstands. I want to be kind to her.

Above us, below us, the ship spins slowly in the night, grinding quietly. From a porthole, Merrett surveys the waters with distrust.

White plastic fibrils appear here and there in the darkness of the ship. They stretch and snap and bud, then break quickly and disappear.

The water comes over, brimming, golden-grey, with nobody to notice it. Full of pale light towards the surface. No more taste to it than to a human body. Broken thistles afloat in it. Lapping softly down the plates of the hull it finds its level again.

In the dawn light, something dark hopping from one wave trough to the next, keeping level with the ship, just as a sunbeam sometimes does. Nothing to bother about.

The ship draws in again the coils of piping that trailed beneath its hull in the night. Far from land, we sail in shallows where grey cylinders and globes lie under the water, near enough to the surface for their rivets to show.

I go below, and feel the ship above me turn, turning, trying to find the night again.

This is what it is like on the land: the town-gods, with coloured rings painted round their eyes, drive their cars down to the water's edge and stand in them watching the ships go by.

Protection has its grip slowly peeled off all of us, and off all our things. We're left glistening and tight. What it is that will taunt, what is it that will lunge?

On the land there are big old sheds of corrugated iron, their reddish-brown paint much faded. Cinder paths behind them, and tough grey-green weeds.

The white iron ceiling, the ivory corner, the washroom door. They have finished in there. The room has been full of steam; the mirrors and walls are clouded over. Damp soiled dressings in the bin. They have gone away. I wonder whether they have forgiven him.

With steam in my glass, a wet clock with fingers that keep slipping back, the effort of propping my shoes against a slippery tiled wall, things are unsteady. Iron ladders lead down, you can see feet, waists, heads moving about. Wiping the moisture off a chromium rim of this chromium-rimmed thing gives a narrow strip of mirror; and glinting, scissor-eyed, they look in from it at what's going on. Two or three of them, not recognisable. Here there are many black shoes, shuffling, swivelling, some of them women's. Wearing at the linoleum.

I smell methylated spirits. Dougal there, just behind me, lying as if dead. He's stripped to the waist but his trousers are neat. Amy, kneeling beside him, pours the stuff on to wadding and wipes his chest and throat. People tread on them in passing. Ducts up into the air, down into the dark. More feet, blackshod, bare pink, thudding close to me along the metal wall beside my ear or across the thick reeded glass lid through which I look up into the bright fog of daylight. High up in it, billows of orange smoke seem to be going past.

Aside to a Children's Tale

This dead march is thin
in our spacious street
as the black procession
that stumbles its beat;

our doors are clerical
and the thin coffin door
winks on a wet pall,
a frozen sore;

and four men like pigs
bear high as they can
the unguarded image
of a private man;

while broken music
lamely goes by
in the drummed earth,
the brassy sky.

Why They Stopped Singing

They stopped singing because
They remembered why they had started

Stopped because
They were singing too well

When they stopped they hoped for
A silence to listen into.

Had they sung longer
The people would not have known what to say.

They stopped from the fear
Of singing for ever

They stopped because they saw the rigid world
Become troubled

Saw it begin
Composing a question.

Then they stopped singing
While there was time.

Toyland

Today the sunlight is the paint on lead soldiers
Only they are people scattering out of the cool church

And as they go across the gravel and among the spring streets
They spread formality: they know, we know, what they have
        been doing,

The old couples, the widowed, the staunch smilers,
The deprived and the few nubile young lily-ladies,

And we know what they will do when they have opened the doors
        of their houses and walked in:
Mostly they will make water, and wash their calm hands and eat.

The organ's flourishes finish; the verger closes the doors;
The choirboys run home, and the rector goes off in his motor.

Here a policeman stalks, the sun glinting on his helmet-crest;
Then a man pushes a perambulator home; and somebody posts a
        letter.

If I sit here long enough, loving it all, I shall see the District
        Nurse pedal past,
The children going to Sunday School and the strollers strolling;

The lights darting on in different rooms as night comes in;
And I shall see washing hung out, and the postman·delivering
        letters.

I might by exception see an ambulance or the fire brigade
Or even, if the chance came round, street musicians (singing and
  playing).

For the people I've seen, this seems the operation of life:
I need the paint of stillness and sunshine to see it that way.

The secret laugh of the world picks them up and shakes them like
  peas boiling;
They behave as if nothing happened; maybe they no longer notice.

I notice. I laugh with the laugh, cultivate it, make much of it,
But still I don't know what the joke is, to tell them.

The Hospital in Winter

A dark bell leadens the hour,
  the three-o'-clock
light falls amber across a tower.

Below, green-railed within a wall
  of coral brick,
stretches the borough hospital

monstrous with smells that cover death,
  white gauze tongues,
cold-water-pipes of pain, glass breath,

porcelain, blood, black rubber tyres;
  and in the yards
plane trees and slant telephone wires.

On benches squat the afraid and cold
  hour after hour.
Chains of windows snarl with gold.

Far off, beyond the engine-sheds,
  motionless trucks
grow ponderous, their rotting reds

deepening towards night; from windows
          bathrobed men
watch the horizon flare as the light goes.

Smoke whispers across the town,
          high panes are bleak;
pink of coral sinks to brown;
a dark bell brings the dark down.

As He Came Near Death

As he came near death things grew shallower for us:
We'd lost sleep and now sat muffled in the scent of tulips, the
          medical odours, and the street sounds going past, going
          away;
And he, too, slept little, the morphine and the pink light the
          curtains let through floating him with us,
So that he lay and was worked out on to the skin of his life and
          left there,
And we had to reach only a little way into the warm bed to scoop
          him up.

A few days, slow tumbling escalators of visitors and cheques, and
          something like popularity;
During this time somebody washed him in a soap called *Narcissus*
          and mounted him, frilled with satin, in a polished case.

Then the hole: this was a slot punched in a square of plastic grass
          rug, a slot lined with white polythene, floored with dyed
          green gravel.
The box lay in it; we rode in the black cars round a corner, got out
          into our coloured cars and dispersed in easy stages.

After a time the grave got up and went away.

After Working

I like being tired,
to go downhill from waking
late in the day
when the clay hours
have mostly crossed the town
and sails smack on the reservoir
bright and cold;

I squat there by the reeds
in dusty grass near earth
stamped to a zoo patch
fed with dog dung,
and where swifts
flick sooty feathers along the water
agape for flies.

The thoughts I'm used to meeting
at head-height when I walk or drive
get lost here in the petrol haze
that calms the elm-tops
over the sunset shadows I sit among;

and I watch the sails,
the brick dam,
the far buildings brighten,
pulled into light,
sharp edges and transient,
painful to see:

signal to leave looking and
shaded, to fall away
lower than dulled water reaches,
still breathing the dog odour
of water, new flats, suburb trees,
into the half light of a night garage
without a floor,

then down its concrete stems,
shaded as I go down
past slack and soundless
shores of what might be other
scummed waters,
to oil-marked asphalt
and, in the darkness, to a sort of grass.

Seven Attempted Moves

If the night were not so dark
       this would be seen
Deep red,
       the last red before black.
Beside the soft earth steps
       a wall of heaped stones
Breathes and
       flowers
and breathes.

       *

A cast concrete basin
       with a hole in the bottom
Empty but for
       a drift of black grit
Some feathers some hair
       some grey paper.
Nothing else for the puzzled face to see.

       *

Crisis –
       a man should be able
To hope for a well made crisis,
Something to brace against.

But see it come in rapidly and mean
            along some corridor
In a pauperous civic Office.

                    *

Under the portico
Huge-winged shadows
            hang
Brown, with a scent
            of powdered leather.
Up the steps
            into this
Depth. Recession.
Promise of star-scratched dark.

Then put your ear to the door;
            listen
As in a shell
            to the traffic
Slithering along behind it.

                    *

Here are the schoolroom chairs on which
            the ministers, in the playground,
Sat to be shot.
            Four chairs; the property
Of the Department of Education;
Stolen
            the same night
By this souvenir hunter
            with his respect for neither side –
Just for things happening;
            then sought in vain
And after a long while
            written off the books
Of the Department of Education.

                    *

Bright birchleaves, luminous and orange,
Stick after six months to the street,
                  trodden down;
Now, as at every minute, perfect.

                    *

It is a shame. There is
                  nowhere to go.
Doors into further in
                  lead out already
To new gardens
Small enough for pets' droppings
                  quickly to cover:
Ceilings
                  too soon, steps curtailed;
The minibed; minibath;
                  and jammed close
                  the minican.

Confinement,
                  shortness of breath.
Only a state of mind.
                  And
Statues of it built everywhere.

For Realism

For 'realism':
the sight of Lucas's
lamp factory on a summer night;
a shift coming off about nine,
pale light, dispersing,
runnels of people chased,
by pavements drying off
quickly after them,
away among the wrinkled brown houses
where there are cracks for them to go;

sometimes, at the corner of Farm and Wheeler Streets,
standing in that stained, half-deserted place

– pale light for staring up
four floors high
through the blind window walls
of a hall of engines,
shady humps left alone,
no lights on in there
except the sky –

there presses in
– and not as conscience –
what concentrates down in the warm hollow:

plenty of life there still,
the foodshops open late, and people
going about constantly, but not far;

there's a man in a blue suit
facing into a corner,
straddling to keep his shoes dry;
women step, talking, over the stream,
and when the men going by call out, he answers.

Above, dignity. A new precinct
comes over the scraped hill,
flats on the ridge get the last light.

Down Wheeler Street, the lamps
already gone, the windows have
lake stretches of silver
gashed out of tea green shadows,
the after-images of brickwork.

A conscience
builds, late, on the ridge. A realism
tries to record, before they're gone,
what silver filth these drains have run.

The Memorial Fountain

The fountain plays
              through summer dusk in gaunt shadows,
black constructions
              against a late clear sky,
water in the basin
              where the column falls
       shaking,
rapid and wild,
              in cross-waves, in back-waves,
       the light glinting and blue,
as in a wind
              though there is none,
                            Harsh
skyline!
              Far-off scaffolding
bitten against the air.

              Sombre mood
in the presence of things,
              no matter what things;
respectful sepia.

       This scene:
       people on the public seats
       embedded in it, darkening
       intelligences of what's visible;
       private, given over, all of them –

Many scenes.

Still sombre.

As for the fountain:
              nothing in the describing
beyond what shows
              for anyone;
       above all
no 'atmosphere'.
              It's like this often –
I don't exaggerate.

And the scene?
a thirty-five-year-old man,
poet,
                by temper, realist,
watching a fountain
and the figures round it
in garish twilight,
                        working
to distinguish an event
from an opinion;
                        this man,
intent and comfortable –

Romantic notion.

From an English Sensibility

There's enough wind
to rock the flower-heads
enough sun
to print their shadows
on the creosoted rail.

Already
this light shaking-up
rouses the traffic noise
out of a slurred riverbed
and lifts voices
as of battered aluminium cowls
toppling up;
black
drive chains racking the hot tiles.

Out in the cokehouse
cobweb
a dark mat
draped on the rubble in a corner
muffled

with a fog of glittering dust
that shakes
captive
in the sunlight
over pitted silver-grey
ghost shapes that shine through.

FROM **MATRIX**

(1971)

In Touch

I took down *Pictures from Brueghel*
                    to see what ways Doc
Williams had of taking off
                    into a poem

                    a strong
                    odour of currants
rose from the pages –

well that was one way.

The Making of the Book

'Let the Blurb be strong,
modest and true.
Build it to take a belting;
they'll pick on that.

Then choose your second gang –
the first, led by your publisher,
you already belong to,
its membership involuntary, if free –

for the other, set up an interesting
tension between the acknowledgements
and the resemblances; but in the photograph keep
the cut of your moustache equivocal.

Write your own warrant. Make plain
in idiot-sized letters
for which of the others you'll take the blame – Yes:
it's *necessary* to belong;

several allegiances
are laid out for you ready.
And remember, though you're only a poet,
there's somebody, somewhere, whose patience

it falls to *you* finally to exhaust.
For poetry, we have to take it, is essential,
though menial; its purpose
constantly to set up little enmities.

Faction makes a reciprocal
to-and-fro of the simplest sort – and characterless
but for an 'aesthetic' variable,
inaudible to all but the players.

And this little mindless motion,
that nobody but the selfless and Schooled-
for-Service would ever stoop to,
drives the Society.
It's a long story:
but the minuscule dialectic,
tick-tacking away, no more than notional,
in obscure columns,

at length transmits itself
mysteriously through Education –
which pays off the poets too,
one way and another –

out beyond Government,
past Control and Commodity
even to the hollowness
of the seventeenth percentile, the outermost
reaches of the responsible.

If the reviewers fall idle, everybody drops dead:
it's as simple as that.

– *Go, little book.*'

Poem

The small
poem
the unit of feeling

Pretty red mouth
blotted and
asking why

Here is your photograph
It is a square
view of the air of things
one certain hour –

when just in the background
a green engine goes mad in a tree
to the end of time, pretty mouth.

FROM THE CUT PAGES

(1971)

Metamorphoses

1

She sleeps, in the day, in the silence. Where there is light, but little else: the white covers, the pillow, her head with its ordinary hair, her forearm dark over the sheet.

She sleeps and it is hardly a mark on the stillness; that she should have moved to be there, that she should be moving now across her sleep as the window where the light comes in passes across the day.

Her warmth is in the shadows of the bed, and the bed has few shadows, the sky is smoked with a little cloud, there are fish-trails high in the air. Her sleep rides on the silence, it is an open mouth travelling backward on moving waves.

Mouth open across the water, the knees loosened in sleep; dusks of the body shadowed around the room. In the light from the window there is the thought of a beat, a flicker, an alternation of aspect from the outside to the inside of the glass. The light is going deep under her.

Enough depth. To clear and come free. There is no taste in the water, there are no edges under it: falling away, the soft mumbled hollows and mounds of marble, veined with brown, a lobby floor gone down into the descending levels of a sea-basin. The sleep comes naked.

Rising through the clear fluid, making their own way, the dragging wisps of brown that were secret hairs or the frame of a print on the wall. And light that cracks into the bubbles near the surface, lighting them like varnish bubbles, breaking them into the silent space between the surface and the curved roof, threaded with moving reflections of water light.

Water lights crossing and combining endlessly over the inward membrane of the roof, rising in a curve, almost a cone, to the round lantern with its dirty panes. The water lights beating silently under the steep slates of the case, under the painted frames of the lantern's windows and the domed lead cap, holding into the sky a two-foot fluted spike.

The cat's glinting face as it stared up between its paws from the odd soft position, near-supine, into which the other cat had rolled it. The other cat was already indifferent, turned away to lick its upthrust leg, but this cat, for the moment, had no next thing.

The cat's glinting face, all mask, no signal, was an old face: on a man it would have been frozen, the defiance of something contemptible. It was framed in soft paws. It stared indiscriminately up at the lights. The cat's eyes, further away than eyes look, more distance in them, no cat. Running in to the distance there's a dull aluminium strip of road, tall skies, flat horizons, with scattered elms and poplars picked out in colour by the sun.

All the green fields are cold, the bright afternoon deserted. Faces look out of the cars that go by; that is what they do, those faces. There is a tower among the trees, a white drum on legs, and a road turns off beside it, sweeping down to a cinder patch by the river where the field-tracks join and cars can park. A path, much mauled and trodden, leads through the elders, and at one place, where it crosses a marshy dip, a sheet of corrugated iron has been wedged, balanced on a springy root and half earthed over.

3

How does he come to be wearing that suit, clay-coloured, with a hang-off jacket and flapping trousers that make him seem to jerk? He's making for the ferry; no he's not. He stands a while and goes somewhere else.

A man among the puddles with his shoes on the pavement and his head in the clear air, his nervous system shrouded in loose, dried-looking clothes. His trajectory leads these arrangements he has to a pause, then takes them past it. While he is there and after he's gone, the shut car-park kiosk remains unwaveringly present.

For a few seconds in the centre of a rigidly composed scene, its elements stopped in the act of crossing from left to right or right to left, there is, maybe in the name of freedom, maybe in the name of compulsion, an unidentified capering, that leaves no trace after it has gone. The pavement gives place immediately to the air above it; there was the sign of a thing like a man in the air, an eddy across the scene.

No system describes the world. The fixures moving in the background stop and wait in mid-step, the sound-track cuts out: the projector motor runs on, the beam doesn't waver. Among the whites and greys of the picture a golden shade is born, in the quiet, rippling slowly, knotting itself and suddenly swelling into a cauliflower head, amber and cream cumulus outlined in blistering magenta, erupting out of itself and filling the screen before shrivelling off upwards to leave a blank screen and a stink of fire.

4

Red beans in to soak. A thickness of them, almost brimming the glass basin, swelling and softening together, the colour of their husks draining out to a fog of blood in the water.

The mass of things, indistinguishable one from another, loosing their qualities into the common cloud, their depth squashed by the refraction and obscured in the stain, forms pushed out of line. Five beans down it may be different.

Down in the levels, it's possible to think outward to the edge; with a face to the light, there's no looking out, only hunching before the erosion. Back!

In the midst is neither upward nor downward, head nor foot has precedence or order. Curved belly rises above, warm and shining, its navel out on surface with the vestige of a lip. One eye is enough, to distinguish shape from shadow, paired eyes would fix too much. To be fixed in the midst is suffocation.

So, in the thick of the world, watching the moon whiten the bedroom floor and drag the print of the window nets higher and higher across the wall; thinking how the world would have had a different history if there had always been not one moon in the sky, but a close-set pair. It is said there are two breasts; it is said there are two sexes. That's as may be.

Out in the moonlight is a short street with only one side; houses on it, and walled forecourts. Over the way is a white pavement, and a blackness where the hill falls away. The blackness goes grey with looking, and the valley is full of shapes.

FROM THE THING ABOUT
JOE SULLIVAN

(1978)

The Thing About Joe Sullivan

The pianist Joe Sullivan,
jamming sound against idea

hard as it can go
florid and dangerous

slams at the beat, or hovers,
drumming, along its spikes;

in his time almost the only
one of them to ignore

the chance of easing down,
walking it leisurely,

he'll strut, with gambling shapes,
underpinning by James P.,

amble, and stride over
gulfs of his own leaving, perilously

toppling octaves down to where
the chords grow fat again

and ride hard-edged, most lucidly
voiced, and in good inversions even when

the piano seems at risk of being
hammered the next second into scrap.

For all that, he won't swing
like all the others;

disregards mere continuity,
the snakecharming business,

the 'masturbator's rhythm'
under the long variations:

Sullivan can gut a sequence
in one chorus –

– approach, development, climax, discard –
and sound magnanimous.

The mannerism of intensity
often with him seems true,

too much to be said, the mood
pressing in right at the start, then

running among stock forms
that could play themselves

and moving there with such
quickness of intellect

that shapes flaw and fuse,
altering without much sign,

concentration
so wrapped up in thoroughness

it can sound bluff, bustling,
just big-handed stuff –

belied by what drives him in
to make rigid, display,

shout and abscond, rather
than just let it come, let it go –

And that thing is his mood
a feeling violent and ordinary

that runs in among standard forms so
wrapped up in clarity

that fingers following his
through figures that sound obvious

find corners everywhere,
marks of invention, wakefulness;

the rapid and perverse
tracks that ordinary feelings

make when they get driven
hard enough against time.

From the *Town Guide*

Out in the air, the statue
gets cold. It needs a coat.

The coat must have a face on top
to squint for dandruff on the shoulder.

It always did have trousers,
Remember? And a wife.

– She was a raver, great big
wardroby body. Insatiable. Still is.

She drives a car like that one
by the Conveniences. His epitaph

Stands all about. But on his plinth
read simply: 'The Unknown Alderman'.

The Least

The least, the meanest,
goes down to less;
there's never an end.

And you can learn
looking for less
and again, less;
your eyes don't get sharper.

For there is less
eyesight;
and no end to that.

There is you,
there is less-you:
the merest trace –
less-eyes will find it.

Artists, Providers, Places to Go

The little figures in the architect's drawing
the sleep of reason begets
little figures.

Nose the car up through the ramps
into a bay, and leave it,
keys in the dash by regulation –
cost-effective:
come back and find it gone,
you got free parking.

The concrete multi-tiers
on the high-rise estate
hold everybody's wagon.

Only they don't. What's left there
their kids tear apart, Monkeyville –
anybody in their right mind would have known it.

Next, the Adventure Playground.

Next, celibate adult males
shipped in from the Homelands for work
sleep on long shelves of concrete,
Unity of Habitation. No damp.

– for that drawing, reduce
Sleepers in the Underground to cosiness,
consider the blanket concession.

And there'll always be a taker
for a forgotten corner out of Brueghel
suitable for a bare-buttocked, incontinent,
sunken-cheeked ending. Little figure
settled in there.

The Sign

First I saw it in colour, then I killed it.
What was still moving, I froze.
That came away. The colour all went
to somebody else's heaven, may they
live on in blessedness. What
came to my hand was fragile, beautiful
and grey, a photograph twilight;
so little to decay there, yet it would
be going down, slowly, be
going down.

Epitaph: Lorine Niedecker

Certain trees
came separately from the wood

and with no special
thought of returning

Occasional Poem 7.1.72

The poets are dying because they are told to die.
What kind of dirt is that? Whose hand
jiggles the nerve, what programme demands it,
what death-train are we on? Not poetry:
some of us drink,
some take the wrong kind of walk
or get picked up in canteens
by killer lays – it's all
tasteless to talk about.
Taste is what death has for the talented? Then
the civilisation is filth, its taste
the scum on filth. Then the poets
are going to be moving on out past talent,
out past taste. If taste
gets its gift wrappers on death – well –
out past that, too. There are courts
where nobody ought to testify.

Commuter

Shallow, dangerous, but without sensation:
sun beats in the rear view mirror
with cars squatting in the glare
and coming on. This continues.
Gasholders flicker along the horizon.

Out in all weathers on the test rig
that simulates distance by substituting
a noise drawn between two points;
shallow, my face printed on the windscreen,
profile on the side glass; shallow —

Either I have no secrets
or the whole thing's a secret
I've forgotten to tell myself:
something to make time for on the night run south,
when the dazzle turns to clear black
and I can stare out over the wheel
straight at Orion, printed on the windscreen.

Inscriptions for Bluebeard's Castle
(for Ronald King)

The Portcullis

Beyond me the common daylight
divides

The Castle

The furthest journey is the journey that stays still
and the light of the sky has come from the world
to be packed for a journey

The Instruments of Torture

Man conceived us, men made us. We work
almost with perfection and we feel no pain.

The Armoury

Provide. That their mouths may bleed into the cinders.
With bronze and steel, provide. With beauty, provide.

The Treasure House

What
the sun touches
shines on forever dead
the dead images of the sun
wonderful

The Garden

Whose is the body you
remember in yourself?

The Land

The light. The rain. The eye. The rainbow –
horizons form, random and inevitable as rainbows
over bright fields of change

The Lake of Tears

Day has turned to a silver mirror
whose dead extent the weeping
eyes could never see

The Last Door

Moonlight the dead image of the day –
here by the light of that last coin
we are alive within an eye:
when the eye closes on us all
it is complete

107 Poems

(Pentameters for Eric Mottram)

A scraping in the cokehouse. One red car.
Imperfect science weakens assurances
but swallowing hard brings confidence: fall soft
through to a sunlit verge. Another vision:
stretched out like one expecting autopsy
or showers of sparks across a polished hall.

Swallow all down, to mudstains on the glass;
surmounted by the working, come upon
a sweet for Auntie; for the withdrawn and hurt
something comes sloping upwards, tilts the guard,
then goes across another way: surprise
relaxes from a sideboard in a bottle,
rocks to and fro a while, scores up another –
bottle between the lips – is comforted
into a pointless trip and passes out
finally between two stations, wrapped in yellow.

Sepia slippers in a sepia print,
venerable truth again: it comes direct
and broadens as it comes, is beautiful
if truth is what you want; lies in the blood
and lives on without taint. Magnificent
gorges at sunset! They knew how to live.
They draw us in their footsteps, double-tongued.

To drive under the fog again, and to it,
park by red lights along the road gang's ditch;
changes of *Satin Doll* are getting smothered,
two trumpets and a rhythm section working

carelessly through a roof under the ground;
at twenty past the hour they hit the dirt,
go on across the talk, hit it some more;
a silver surface rears up, wonderful;
somebody scared runs in and turns it over.

Squatting resigned among the rest of it
there's cut and come again; eat anything.
Demolished streets make foregrounds to good skies;
warm hands at rubbish fires, or on a keyboard.
But brightness picks out streaks of signal red,
it's morning. Rumpled, nobody can cope.
What leaks through rotted pipes into the gutter
leaves a long stain that tired arms cannot move,
dispirited by sickness and privation
when peaceful hours have coal dumped under them,
a last delivery, ferried in through sleet.

What's newly made gets treated tenderly;
damage is easy while the aconite
first shows under the window's overhang
and looks well. In the cold light is a refuge,
lying back after breakfast to see birds
flash down the pale grey strip beyond the roof;
and it's a lime-green tent where everything
is fugitive and found, and luminous,
with shadows of a dark track off the calendar
into a depth of sky. Hanging there free,
spiralling down, the ink-trails in the water
that reach the floor and spread. To be well-treated –
a café with net curtains where they bring
coffee or coca-cola to the bedridden –
something to recall on a beleaguered common.
Roads open in succession, windows break;
if both your legs get tired, find a good stick;
slow before lunch, but in the afternoons
Olympic stars perform for invalids
and dark brings in harsh winds and roadside breakdowns;
better to hear of rain on other roofs
or technicolour wrongs worked by hard men.

No choice left but to run, and into it
and back again each time, that being where

102

the way goes anyhow – so, running
brings it round so much faster, the same dream –
daffodil plastic, various laminates,
children released in yards then sucked away
into an unseen hall; enormous tolerance
somewhere about, and for immediate sky,
hand-lotion-coloured plastic overhead,
the first thing in the world; and back again.
Walking across to the cars in the night air,
everyone slows and vanishes. There'll be
familiar movement when the season dives.
Watch ampelopsis redden the tarred wall;
go straight, and not so fast. The inner sky
is coloured plastic – none the worse for it.

Somewhere the copper pipes a pale gasfitter
left unsecured under the floor tread loose.
The new face might look younger were it not
too harried and too sleepy: there's no time.
Old people go so childish you get scared
thinking about it: someone's moving out.
Under the trees, headlands of alyssum
break through a spring where danger without risk
develops to a style and loses body,
loses its ear for trouble. Ride again.
Desolate sunlit foreshores, visited
and photographed, lie doubly far away;
one more red car gets dealt into the pack;
one guest is laid to rest in his own nature,
his to resist if it should overcome him
travelling in the tracks of a clay lorry
or when the powercut lets the dark back in.

Exhausted, by a different route, twice blessed –
they seem like wooden roses, without yield –
draining the glass again, whatever remains,
past all surprise, repeatedly and strong
though without strength, except to head on out,
surrounded by a street, braced up to feel,
ready for thunder, inescapable change,
the healing of the injured; some idea
of what tradition numbers like these are benched in.

Sets

If you take a poem
you must take another
and another
till you have a poet.

And if you take a poet
you'll take another, and so on,
till finally you get
a civilisation: or just
the dirtiest brawl you ever saw –
the choice isn't yours.

Timelessness of Desire

Into the purpose: or out.
There is only, without a tune,
timelessness of desire.

don't open up the way
this town shines in through glass
and the days darken;
there's nothing better,
not one thing better to do –

What's now only disproved
was once imagined.

A Poem Not a Picture

On a ground remarkable for lack of character, sweeps of direction form.

It's not possible to determine whether they rise from the ground's qualities or are marked on to it. Or whether, if the first, the lines suck the ground's force up, or are its delegates; or if the second, whether the imposed marks mobilise or defeat it; or both, in all cases.

Out of a scratch ontology the sweeps of direction form, and, as if having direction, produce, at wide intervals, the events.

These are wiry nodes made of small intersecting planes as if rendered by hatching, and having a vapid, played-out look. But they are the nearest the field has to intense features. Each has a little patch of red.

Cut Worm

You're the invention
I invented once before –
I had forgotten.

        I need to invent you now
more than you need to be remembered.

Dark on Dark

Dark on dark –
they never merge:

the eye imagines to separate them,
imagines to make them one:

imagines the notion of impossibility
for eyes.

The Only Image

Salts work their way
to the outside of a plant pot
and dry white.

              This encrustation
is the only image.
            The rest –
the entire winter, if there's winter –
comes as a variable that shifts
in any part, or vanishes.

                I can
compare what I like to the salts,
to the pot, if there's a pot,
to the winter if there's a winter.

The salts I can compare
to anything there is.
Anything.

Emblem
(for Basil Bunting)

Wing
       torn out of stone
like a paper fan

Hung in a sky
         so hard
the stone seems paper

Bare stems of ivy
         silver themselves
into the stones

And hold up the wall
         like an armature
till they force it apart

Dusk

The sun sets
in a wall that holds the sky.

You'll not
be here long, maybe.

The window
filled with reflections
turns on its pivot;

beyond its edge
the air goes on cold and deep;
your hand feels it,
or mine, or both;
it's the same air for ever.

Now reach across the dark.

Now touch the mountain.

It is Writing

Because it could do it well
the poem wants to glorify suffering.
I mistrust it.

I mistrust the poem in its hour of success,
a thing capable of being
tempted by ethics into the wonderful.

The Poet's Message

What sort of message –
what sort of man
comes in a message?

I would
get into a message if I could
and come complete
to where I can see
what's across the park:
and leave my own position
empty for you in its frame.

Of the Empirical Self and for Me
(for M.E.)

In my poems there's seldom
any *I* or *you* –

> you know me, Mary;
> you wouldn't expect it of me –

The night here is humid:
there are two of us sitting out
on the bench under the window;

> two invisible ghosts
> lift glasses of white milk
> and drink
>   and the lamplight
stiffens the white fence opposite.

A tall man passes
with what looks like a black dog.
He stares at the milk, and says
> *It's nice to be able*
> *to drink a cup of*
> *coffee outside at night...*

and vanishes. So –
What kind of a world? Even
love's not often a poem. The night
has to move quickly. Sudden rain.
Thunder bursts across the mountain;
the village goes dark with blown fuses,
and lightning-strokes repeatedly
bang out their own reality-prints
of the same white houses
staring an instant out of the dark.

Barnardine's Reply

Barnardine, given his life back,
is silent.

       With such conditions
what can he say?

         The talk
is all about mad arrangements, the owners
counting on their fingers,
calling it discourse, cheating,
so long as the light increases,
the prisms divide and subdivide,
the caverns crystallise out into day.

Barnardine,
whose sole insight into time
is that the right day for being hanged on
doesn't exist,
         is given
the future to understand.

It comes
as a free sample from the patentholders;
it keeps him quiet for a while.

It's not the reprieve in itself
that baffles him:
he smelt that coming
well before justice devised it –
              lords
who accept the warrant,
put on a clean shirt,
walk to the scaffold,
shake hands all round,
forgive the headsman,
kneel down and say, distinctly, 'Now!' attract
pickpockets of the mind –

But he's led away
not into the black vomit pit
he came out of
but into a dawn world
of images without words
where armed men, shadows in pewter,
ride out of the air and vanish,
and never once stop to say what they mean:

– thumb with a broken nail
starts at the ear lobe,
traces the artery down,
crosses the clavicle, circles
the veined breast with its risen nipple,
goes down under the slope of the belly,
stretching the skin after it –

butchered just for his stink,
and for the look in his eye –

In the grey light of a deserted barn
the Venus, bending to grip the stone sill,
puts up no case for what she's after,
not even a sigh,
but flexes her back.
                        No choice for the Adonis
but to mount her wordlessly, like a hunting dog –
    just for her scent
    and for the look in her eye.

Somebody draws
a Justice
on the jail wall;

gagged with its blindfold
and wild about the eyes.

If I Didn't

If I didn't dislike
mentioning works of art

I could say
the poem has always
already started, the parapet
snaking away, its grey line guarding
the football field and the sea

– the parapet
has always already started
snaking away, its grey line
guarding the football field and the sea

and under whatever progression
takes things forward

there's always
the looking down
between the moving frames

into those other movements
made long ago or in some
irrecoverable scale
but in the same alignment
and close to recall.

Some I don't recognise,
but I believe them –

one system of crimson scaffolding,
another, of flanges –

All of them must be mine,
the way I move on:

and there I am,
half my lifetime back,
on Goodrington sands
one winter Saturday,

troubled in mind: troubled
only by Goodrington beach
under the gloom, the look of it
against its hinterland

and to be walking
acres of sandy wrack,
sodden and unstable
from one end to the other.

Paraphrases

(for Peter Ryan)

Dear Mr Fisher I am writing
a thesis on your work.
But am unable to obtain
texts. I have articles by Davie, D.,
and Mottram, E.,
but not your Books since booksellers
I have approached refuse to
take my order saying they
can no longer afford to
handle 'this type of business'. It is
too late! for me to change
my subject to the work of a more
popular writer, so please Mr Fisher
you must help me since I face the alternatives
of failing my degree or repaying
the whole of my scholarship money...

Dear Mr Fisher although I have been unable
to read much of your work (to get it that is)
I am a great admirer of it and your landscapes
have become so real to me I am convinced I have, in fact,
become you. I have never, however,
seen any photograph of you, and am most curious
to have an idea of your appearance,
beyond what my mirror, of course, tells me.

The cover of your *Collected Poems*
(reproduced in the *Guardian*, November 1971)
shows upwards of fifty faces; but which is yours? Are you
the little boy at the front, and if so have you
changed much since then?

Dear Mr Fisher recently while studying
selections from a modern anthology with
one of my GCE groups I came across your interestingly titled
'Starting to Make a Tree'. After the discussion I felt strongly
you were definitely *holding something back* in this poem
though I can't quite reach it. Are you often in Rugby?
If you are, perhaps we could meet and I could
try at least to explain. Cordially, Avis Tree. PS. Should we
arrange a rendezvous I'm afraid I wouldn't
know who to look out for as I've never unfortunately
seen your photograph. But I notice you were born in 1930
the same year as Ted Hughes. Would I be right
in expecting you to resemble *him*, more or less?

                              – Dear Ms Tree,
It's true I'm in Rugby quite often, but the train
goes through without stopping. Could you fancy standing
outside the UP Refreshment Room a few times so that
I could learn to recognise *you*? If you could
just get hold of my four books, and wave them
then I'd know it was you. As for my own appearance
I suppose it inclines more to the
Philip Larkin side of Ted Hughes's looks...
See if you think so as I go by...

Dear Mr Fisher I have been commissioned
to write a short
critical book on your work
but find that although I have a full
dossier of reviews etcetera
I don't have access to your books. Libraries
over here seem just not to have bought them in.
Since the books are quite a few years old now
I imagine they'll all have been remaindered
some while back? Or worse, pulped? So can
you advise me on locating second-hand copies,
not too expensively I hope? Anyway,
yours, with apologies and respect...

Dear Mr Fisher I am now
so certain I am you that it is obvious to me
that the collection of poems I am currently working on
            must be
your own next book! Can you let me know –
who is to publish it and exactly when
it will be appearing? I shouldn't like there to
be any trouble over contracts, 'plagiarism'
etcetcra; besides which it would be a pity
to think one of us was wasting time and effort.
How far have *you* got? Please help me. I
do think this is urgent...

Diversions

1

Trouble coming, on a Saturday or a Monday,
some day with a name to it:

staining the old paths trouble knows,
though I forget them.

2

Walk through, minding the nettles
at the corner of the brick path –

don't feel sorry for language, it doesn't bear
            talking about.

3

Built for quoting in a tight corner –
The power of dead imaginings to return.

4

Just beside my track through the dark,
my own dark, not to be described,
the screech-owl
sounds, in his proper cry
and in all his veritable image –
you would know him at once.

Beyond him
a dissolution of my darkness
into such forms
as live there in the space
beyond the clear image of an owl:

forms without image;
pointless to describe.

5

I saw what there was to write and I wrote it.
When it felt what I was doing, it lay down and died under me.

6

Grey weather beating across the upland,
and the weather matters.
Grey weather beating easily across the upland.

7

Crooked-angle wings
blown sideways
against the edge of the picture.

8

Roused from a double
depth of sleep, looking up
through a hole in the sleep's surface above;
no sense of what's there;
a luminous dial
weaves along the dark like a torch.
There's somebody already
up and about, a touch-paper crackle
to their whispering.

9

The kites are the best sort of gods,
mindless, but all style;

even their capriciousness,
however dominant,
not theirs at all.

Lost from its line
one flies steadily out to sea,
its printed imperturbable face
glinting as it dips and rises
dwindling over the waves.

The crowd on the shore
reach out their hearts.

10

Leaden August with the life gone out of it,
not enough motion
to shift old used-up things.

A bad time to be rid of troubles,
they roll back in.

Dead troubles take longer than live ones.

11

The pilgrim disposition –
walking in strung-out crowds
on exposed trackways
as if ten yards from home:

domestic to-ing and fro-ing
uncoiled and elongated
in a dream of purpose.

12

Then some calm and formal portrait
to turn a level gaze
on the milling notions,

its tawniness of skin denoting
tension maybe, a controlled pallor;

or a blush of self-delight
welling softly from its intelligence.

13

Periodicity: the crack
under the door of this room
as I stare at it, late at night,
has the same relation to its field
as – what?

The corner over the curtain-rail
in a room I was in one night
forty years ago and more.

The light and the height are different,
and so am I;
but something in the staring
comes round again.

So I stare
at the single recurrence of a counter
I expect never to need.

14

Sliding the tongue-leaved
crassula arborescens
smartly in its pot and saucer
from one end of the windowsill
right down to the other

alters the framed view, much
as a louvred shutter would.

All my life I've been left-handed.

15

Here comes the modulation.
Elbows in, tighten up:
a sucked-in, menacing sound,
but full. The space is narrow,
the time marked out,
and everybody's watching.

16

The woman across the lane
stoops, hands on knees,
behind out, black and grey hair
falling forward, her nose level
with the top of a four foot wall
under a huge shaggy bank of privet.

Nose to nose with her across a saucer,
his tail lifting into the privet shadow,
a big dark cat with a man's
face marked out in white.

Quietly,
in a good, firm Scottish voice,
set well down,
she tells his story:
                    how
when his owners first

moved another cat in on him
then moved out altogether,
he ran wild for three years,
haunting back once in a while,
a frightener.

After that
for a year and a half
she'd set for him daily,
slowly drawing him in

as near as this;
she didn't expect more.

She talks, and the cat drinks.
He turns his mask to me,
sees me, and without pausing
vanishes.

      Later, from a distance,
I see the two of them again,
a saucer apart. The cat
with his enormous guilt
and importance;
      the fortunate cat,
to have such a calm Scots lady
to understand his importance.

17

Out to one side
a flight of shops
turning towards the sun,

each one a shallow step higher,
white and new and good.

And there's the ultimate in shops;
the gallery.

Somebody can be stood –
can elect to stand –
in fresh clothes but barefoot
on a slate ledge, in the place of a pot,

fastidious
beyond the flakings of the skin,
the vegetable variants of body-form,
the negative
body-aura,
that shadowy khaki coat.

Can stand, and receive attributions
of pain and excellence.

18

Everything cast in iron
must first be made in wood –

The foundry patternmaker
shapes drains, gears,
furnace doors, couplings
in yellow pine.

His work fulfils the conditions for myth:
it celebrates origin,
it fixes forms for endless recurrence;
it relates energy to form;
is useless in itself;

for all these reasons it also attracts
aesthetic responses in anybody
free to respond aesthetically;

and it can be thought with;

arranged on trays in the Industrial Museum,
it mimes the comportment
of the gods in the Ethnology cases.

19

Outlines
start to appear
on the milky surface.

Points first,
quickening into perimeters
branches and dividers;
an accelerating wonder.

Arrest; try lifting it away
before the creation
diversifies totally
to a deadlocked fission:
diamond-faceted housebricks
in less than light.

The thin trace lifted off will drop
into a new medium and dissolve.
On the bland surface
will appear new outlines.

Both these ways are in nature.

20

A world
arranged in zones
outside and into
this waterfront café.

A strip of sky
misty with light,

a deep band of
dark hazy mountainside,

a whole estuary width
foreshortened almost to nothing,

a quay,
a full harbour;

then a pavement,
a sill,

the table where I sit,
and the darkness in my head.

Everything still along its level

except the middle zone, the harbour water,
turbulent with the sunlight
even in calm air.

The Dirty Dozen

Dirty Nature,
Dirty sea;

Dirty daytime,
Dirty cry;

Dirty melody,
Dirty heart;

Dirty God,
Dirty surprise;

Dirty drumlin,
Dirty design;

Dirty radiance,
Dirty ghost.

3rd November 1976

Maybe twenty of us in the late afternoon
are still in discussion. We're talking
about the Arts Council of Great Britain
and its beliefs about itself. We're baffled.

We're in a hired pale clubroom
high over the County Cricket Ground
and we're a set of darkening heads,
turning and talking and hanging down;

beyond the plate glass, in another system, silent,
the green pitch rears up, all colour,
and differently processed. Across it in olive overalls
three performance artists persistently move
with rakes and rods. The cold sky steepens.
Twilight catches the flats rising out of the trees.

One of our number is abducted
into the picture. A sculptor innocent of bureaucracy
raises his fine head to speak out;
and the window and its world frame him.
He is made clear.

FROM **POEMS 1955-1980**

(1980)

Five Pilgrims in the Prologue to *The Canterbury Tales*

Knight

He bore himself, or the self he had was borne,
through great indignities and darkness
inviolate in a glass braced with silver.
It was as small as that.

In Lithuania, spars and foul fabrics
prised out of black silt with a frozen crack;

elsewhere, excrements rolled in sand;

scattered all across the back of beyond, seedy nobility,
mincing and cheating, and getting cut to pieces.

As often as he set forth, he would find himself
returning through strange farmlands
in incomprehensible weather.

Webbe

Risen by weaving works to this
abstraction: something at the same time
rich and dry about that trade,
a station on the road to pure money;
stretching resources till the patterns glow.

Dyere

Even in the pools
and vats, even in the steamy
swags and folds and leaf-stinks
stuck in the nose at night
there's always been someone's white finger
waving above it all.

Tapicer

Base yourself on these,
Lords. I have slipped
the carpet in under your foot,
the cushion beneath your buttocks;
the walls are all taken care of.

It is with this sort of confidence
you can look me in the eye.

Cook

Slow cooking in a world on the move.
The hours are slow, the pies live a long time;
cooling and warming, they ride the bacterial dumb-waiter.
A cook goes in and out of focus many times as he learns.

On the bright side, the ulcer's almost forgettable,
and the flies loose in the shop don't irritate,
being mostly middle-sized and black, and in no hurry.

Wonders of Obligation

We know that hereabouts
comes into being
the malted-milk brickwork
on its journey past the sun.

The face of its designer
sleeps into a tussocky
field with celandines

and the afternoon
comes on steely and still
under the heat,

with part of the skyline
settling to a dark slate
frieze of chimneys
stiffened to peel away
off the western edge.

I saw
the mass graves dug
the size of workhouse wards
into the clay

ready for most of the people
the air-raids were going to kill:

still at work, still in the fish-queue;
some will have looked down
into their own graves on Sundays

provided
for the poor of Birmingham
the people of Birmingham,
the working people of Birmingham,
the allotment holders and Mother, of Birmingham.
The poor.

Once the bombs got you
you were a pauper:
clay, faeces, no teeth; on a level
with gas mains,
even more at a loss than before,
down in the terraces between the targets,
between the wagon works
and the moonlight on the canal.

A little old woman
with a pink nose, we knew her,
had to go into the pit, dead of pneumonia,
had to go to the pit with the rest,
it was thought shame.

Suddenly to go
to the school jakes with the rest
in a rush by the clock.
What had been strange and inward
become nothing, a piss-pallor
with gabble. Already they were lost,
taught unguessed silliness,
to squirt and squeal there.
What was wrong? Suddenly
to distrust your own class
and be demoralised
as any public-school boy.

The things we make up out of language
turn into common property.
To feel responsible
I put my poor footprint back in.

I preserve
Saturday's afterglow
arched over the skyline road
out of Scot Hay:
the hare
zig-zagging slowly

like the shadow of a hare
away up the field-path

to where the blue
translucent sky-glass
reared from the upland
and back overhead

paling, paling
to the west
and down to the muffled rim of the plain.

As many skies as you can look at
stretched in a second
the manifest
of more forms than anyone could see

and it alters
every second you watch it,
bulking and smearing the inks
around landlocked light-harbours

Right overhead, crane back,
blurred grey tufts of cloud
dyeing themselves blue,
never to be in focus, the glass
marred. Choose this sky. It is
a chosen sky.

What lies
in the mound at Cascob?
The church built into the mound.

In the bell-tower
is in the mound.

                    Stand
in the cold earth with the tower around you
and spy out to the sanctuary
down to whatever lies dead there

under the tiny crimson
lamp of the live corpse of the god.

Later than all that
or at some other great remove
an old gentleman
takes his ease on a shooting stick
by the playground on Wolstanton Marsh.

A sunny afternoon on the grass
and his cheeks are pink,
his teeth are made for a grin; happily
his arms wave free. The two stiff
women he has with him in trousers and anoraks
indicate him. They point
or incline towards him. One
moves a good way along the path, stretching a pattern.
The cars pass
within a yard of him. Even so,
he seems, on his invisible stick, to be sitting
on the far edge of the opposite pavement.
Numerous people
group and regroup as if coldly
on a coarse sheet of green.

Parked here, talking,
I'm pleasurably watchful
of the long
forces angled in.

The first farmyard I ever saw
was mostly midden
a collapse of black
with dung and straw swirls
where the drays swung
past the sagging barn.
Always silent. The house
averted, a poor ailanthus
by its high garden gate and
the lane along the hilltop
a tangle of watery ruts
that shone between holly hedges.
Through the gaps you could see
the ricks glowing yellow.

The other farm I had
was in an old picture book,

deep-tinted idyll with steam
threshers, laughing men,
Bruno the hound with his black muzzle,
and the World's Tabbiest Cat.

Describing Lloyd's farm now
moralises it; as the other
always was. But I swear
I saw them both then
in all their properties,
and to me, the difference was neutral.

As if from a chimney
the laws of the sky go floating
slowly above the trees.

And now the single creature
makes itself seen,
isolate,
is an apparition

Near Hartington
in a limestone defile
the barn owl
flaps from an ash
away through the mournful afternoon
misjudging its moment
its omen undelivered.

The hare
dodging towards the skyline at sunset
with a strange goodwill –
he'll do for you and me.

And *mormo maura*
the huge fusty Old Lady moth
rocking its way up
the outside of the dark pane
brandishing all its legs, its
antennae, whirring wings,
zig-zagging upwards, impelled
to be seen coming in from the night.

Now I have come
through obduracy
discomfort and trouble
to recognise it

                    my life keeps
leaking out of my poetry to me
in all directions. It's untidy
ragged and bright
and it's not
used to things

mormo maura
asleep in the curtain
by day.

Scent on the body
inherent or applied
concentrates the mind
holds it from sidelong wandering.
Even when it repels
it pushes directly.

Streaks of life
awkward
showing among straw tussocks
in shallow flood.

Neither living nor saying
has ceremony or bound.

Now I have come
to recognise it, the alder
concentrates my mind
to the water
under its firm green.

Fetching up with
leaf-gloss against
the river-shine.

I want
to remark formally, indeed

stiffly, though not complaining,
that the place where I was raised
had no longer deference for water
and little of it showing. The Rea,
the city's first river,
meagre and under the streets;
and the Tame
wandering waste grounds,
always behind
some factory or fence.

Warstone Pool in the fields
I realised today was a stream dammed
to make way for the colliery.
Handsworth Park lake, again a dam
on the Saxon's
nameless trickle of a stream
under the church bluff. The brook
nearest home, no more than a mile,
ran straight out into the light
from under the cemetery;
and there the caddis-flies would case
themselves in wondrous grit.

I'm obsessed
with cambered tarmacs, concretes,
the washings of rain.

That there can come a sound
as cold as this across the world
on a black summer night,

the moths out there impermeable,
hooded in their crevices
covered in the sound of the rain
breaking from the eaves-gutters
choked with pine needles;
the slippery needles wash everywhere,
they block the down-spouts;
in the shallow pool on the porch roof,
arranged among dashed pine branches
and trails of needles,
I found two ringdove squabs

drowned and picked clean,
dried to black fins.

Fine edge
or deflection
of my feeling towards
anything that behaves or changes,
however slowly; like
my Bryophyllum *Good Luck*,
raised by me from a life-scrap and
now lurching static from its pot,
its leaves winged
with the mouse-ears of its young.
I'm vehemently and steadily
part of its life.

                  Or it slides
sideways and down, under my suspicion –
Now what's it doing?

Suddenly to distrust
the others' mode;
the others. Poinsettias or moths,
or Kenny and Leslie and Leonard,
Edie and Bernard and Dorothy,
the intake of '35; the story of the Wigan pisspot
of about that time, and even
Coleridge's of long before:

I have to set him
to fill it by candlelight
before he transfigures it;

with *mormo maura* the Old Lady moth
beating on the pane to come in.

The Supposed Dancer

Jumping out of the straw,
jumping out of the straw,
his cheeks alive with bristles,
jumping out –
                    you've got him!
He'll ruin the lot of you,
jumping out:
          two drums
          tied up in this
  jumping
          and the joy and the
jumping
          bitchery of art, the men
          with warm hard
          hearts
                    out of the straw –
Got him!
                    Alive with bristles,
jumping with his cheeks
out of the straw alive
with bristles, his cheeks
          ready to jump
the cameraman's guitar, the guitarist's
          camera;
                    alive with
jumping out of the
jumping out of the straw.

FROM **POEMS 1979-1987**

(1988)

Irreversible

The *Atlantic Review* misspelled Kokoschka.
In three weeks he was dead.

Ninety-three years to build a name –
Kokoschka – but he felt
that fine crack in the glaze.

Then he 'suffered a short illness';
that's what the illness was.
Irreversible.

John Ashbery should watch out.
Hiding as John Ash in Haight-Ashbury
won't help in the clash
of Haight-Asch with John Ashbury;
it's got to happen.

I'm just the maker
of mutant poems. In one
sails became *snails* – try it. With me
Organic Form overproduces. Here's
my poem *The Trace*, that's started
to feed off itself, and breed:

– *silky swallowed hair*
that dried and was
flying in a fan –

Now it's *dined and was*
flying in a fan –

– *sulky squalid whore*
that dined and was
Frying in a fin –

For *Trace* read *Truce*;
for *Bruce*, *Brace*:

– *crying in a fit* –

Chisellers! cut deep
into the firm, glistening
sand –

Norseman pass by!

The Home Pianist's Companion

Clanging along in A-flat
correcting faults,

minding the fifths
and fourths in both hands
and for once
letting the tenths look out
for their own chances,

thinking of Mary Lou,
a lesson to us all,

how she will trench and
trench into the firmness of the music
modestly;

thinking,
in my disorder of twofold sense,
or finding rather
an order thinking for me as I play,
of the look of lean-spoked
railway wagon wheels
clanging on a girder bridge,
chopping the daylight, black
wheel across wheel, spoke

over rim, in behind girder and out
revealing the light, withholding it,
inexorable flickers
of segments in overlap
moving in mean elongate
proportions, the consecutive
fourths of appearances,
harsh gaps, small strong
leverages, never still.

The sour face
on that kind of wheel:
I've known that
ever since I first knew anything;
a primary fact of feeling,
of knowing how
best to look after yourself.

Clanging along in A-flat, and
here they come,
the apports, the arrivals:
fourths, wheel-spokes,
and rapidly the eternal
mask of a narrow-faced cat,
its cornered, cringing intensity
moving me to distraction again.

But into the calm
of a time just after infancy
when most things were still
acceptable

this backward image-trail
projects further
on a straight alignment
across what looked to be emptiness,
checked as void

and suddenly locates the dead,
the utterly forgotten:

primal figure of the line,
primitively remembered,
just a posture of her, an apron,
a gait. Vestigial figure,
neighbouring old woman
gaunt, narrow-faced, closed-in,
acceptable,
soon dead.

Still in the air
haunting the fourths
of A-flat major
with wheels and a glinting cat-face;

reminding me
what it was like to be sure,
before language ever
taught me they were different,
of how some things were the same.

The Whale Knot

Sea-beast for sky-worshippers, the whale
easily absorbs all others.
Colours, languages, creatures, forms. Read
the whale in all the ways clouds
are read. The clouds out of sight
are patterned and inscrutable; chaos
from simple constituents,
form out of simple chaos.

A long-drawn complicity with us all
in the sperm-whale's little eye;
among its cells, somewhere,
land-knowledge, the diverse, our condition.

Decamped into boundless viscosity,
our Absolute,
the whale seems simpler than it is:
as easy water-to-land knot
in the museum sperm-whale's bared
head-bone, alive

as the megaliths are alive, all
the force-lines crossing
within their singular undemanding
forms. Lifted from the whale-head,
a disused quarry
swims, borne on the earth;
its cliffs a moon-cradle,
its waters part of the sky.

A Poem to be Watched

Coming into the world
unprepared

and being then always –
in honour of that
birth and to stay
close to it –
under-provided

and driven to exhibit
over and over again
unpreparedness

habitually
unready to be caught
born

News for the Ear

On a kitchen chair
in the grass at Stifford's Bridge,
the cataracts
still on his eyes,
the poet Bunting
dozed in the afternoon,

bored with the talk
of the state of literature that year,
sinking away under it
to his preferred parish
among old names, long reckonings;

but roused at the sound of good news
and surfacing with a rush,
a grunt of delight
from centuries down: 'What?
Has the novel blown over at last, then?'

The Nation

The national day
had dawned. Everywhere
the national tree was opening its blossoms
to the sun's first rays, and from all quarters
young and old in national costume
were making their way to the original National
Building, where the national standard already
fluttered against the sky. Some breakfasted
on the national dish as they walked, frequently
pausing to greet acquaintances with a heartfelt
exchange of the national gesture. Many
were leading the national animal; others carried it
in their arms. The national bird
flew overhead; and on every side
could be heard the keen strains
or the national anthem, played on
the national instrument.

Where enough were gathered together,
national feeling ran high, and concerted cries of
'Death to the national foe!' were raised.
The national weapon was brandished. Though
festivities were constrained by the size of
the national debt, the national sport was
vigorously played all day
and the national drink drunk.
And from midday till late in the evening
there arose continually from the rear
of the national prison the sounds of the national
method of execution, dealing out rapid
justice to those who had given way
– on this day of all days –
to the national vice.

On the Neglect of Figure Composition

Prelude

Hundreds upon hundreds of years of Lapiths
versus Centaurs; Sabine women abducted
by ferocious male models in nothing but
helmets and little cloaks, the corners
curled on their privates; such fading
mileage out of archaic feuds. It all passed.

But I propose a fresh Matter of Britain,
the parties to be as follows. First,
all those who have come to believe
our profoundest guidance to be
the person and style of His Late
Majesty King Zog of Albania: yes, Zog
of the white yachting uniform, of the pistol
for shooting assassins,
of the plump
princesses, in matching
rig, and sharing his peculiar
gift of being able to make himself appear
rancid when photographed.
                                    All British Zoggists
mimic his dress and demeanour, his small
upturned moustache, the proud
suspicion of his eyes. In times of truce
they hold conventions at weekends
in the hotels of our former
manufacturing towns. They dress up,
eye one another, make wild plans.

Most repugnant to them are
the Ianists; once no more than a small
quasi-theological dream, but lately
more numerous, and moving in the land –
though not, it must be remembered,
given much to travelling. For an Ianist
is far more likely to project, or simply telephone,
his outlook and will, for implementation,

to another in the desired locality; they are
a sort of conceptual cavalry.
The heart of Ianism

lies in a constant meditation upon
The Real Ian. The Real Ian
is neither sportsman nor entertainer
but a part-time polytechnic lecturer
called Trevor Hennessy. He teaches
at two polytechnics, one
in the Midlands, the other in the Home
Counties; and he is not
explicit. Ianists are the most implicit
of all known people.

Sketch for the First Exhibition of the New Heroic Art

'Ianists and Zoggists Resting between Engagements, in Rocky Terrain'

'The Spirit of Queen Geraldine, Borne on a Cloud, Encourages Flagging Zoggists during a Skirmish near Burnley'

Diptych: 'Members of an Ianist Cell Brushing their Crests / Appraising One Another's Crests'

'A Zoggist Cohort of the First Rigour Surprised by Ianist Irregulars'

'Five Ianists Scorning to Interrogate a Captured Zoggist'

'The Zoggist College under Snow'

'Ianists Driving Randomly-Coloured Ford Escorts in Formation on the A1 near Peterborough on a Fine April Morning'

'The Zoggist Acceptance of the Surrender of Weybridge'

'Suburban Panorama Incorporating Zoggists Enacting *Enforced Exile in Reduced Circumstances* and Ianists Enacting *Unacknowledged Supremacy*'

'A Modest Zoggist, Borne Unwillingly in Triumph on his Comrades' Shoulders'

'Zoggists in their Cups'

'Condemned Ianists, Already Blindfolded, Exchange Comments on the Turnout of the Zoggist Firing Party'

'Zoggists Hiding in an Ianist Laundry'

'Ianists Relaxing with their Women. They Sit Silent in a Circle Drinking White Rum while their Women Dance Quietly to Records in the Other Half of the Room'

'*The First Time in his Whites*. The Mother of a Zoggist Cadet Proudly Puts the Finishing Touches to his Uniform'

'An Ianist Foraging Party Mingling with the Crowds in Sainsburys'

'Oxford Zoggists in the High'

'The Passage of The Real Ian through Purley by Night'

A FURNACE

(1986)

to the memory of
JOHN COWPER POWYS
(1872-1963)

Introit

November light low and strong
crossing from the left
finds this archaic
trolleybus, touches the side of it up
into solid yellow and green.

This light is without
rarity, it is an oil,
amber and clear that binds in
this alone and suggests
no other. It is a pressing
medium, steady to a purpose.

And in the sun's ray through the glass
lifting towards low noon, I
am bound;
          boots on the alloy
fenders that edge the deck,
lost out of the day
between two working calls
and planted alone
above the driver's head.
High over the roadway
I'm being swung out
into an unknown crosswise
route to a connection
at the Fighting Cocks
by way of Ettingshall;

old industrial road,
buildings to my left along the flat
wastes between townships
wrapped in the luminous

haze underneath the sun,
their forms cut clear and combined
into the mysteries, their surfaces
soft beyond recognition;

and as if I was made
to be the knifeblade, the light-divider,
to my right the brilliance strikes out perpetually
into the brick house-fields towards Wolverhampton,
their calculable distances
shallow with detail.

*

What is it, this
sensation as of freedom? Tang of
town gas, sulphur, tar,
settled among the heavy
separate houses behind
roadside planes, pale, patch-barked
and almost bare,
the last wide stiffened leaves
in tremor across their shadows
with trolley-standards of green cast iron
reared among them, the catenaries
stretching a net just over my guided head,
its roof of yellow metal.

A deserted, sun-battered theatre
under a tearing sky
is energy, its date 19□02
spread across its face, mark of
anomaly. And the road
from Bilston to Ettingshall begins
beating in. Whatever
approaches my passive taking-in,
then surrounds me and goes by
will have itself understood only
phase upon phase
by separate involuntary
strokes of my mind, dark
swings of a fan-blade
that keeps a time of its own,
made up from the long
discrete moments
of the stages of the street,
each bred off the last as if by
causality.

Because
of the brick theatre struck to the roadside
the shops in the next
street run in a curve, and
because of that there is raised up
with red lead on its girders
a gasworks
close beyond the roofs,

and because of he fold of the
folding in of these three to me
there comes a frame tower with gaps
in its corrugated cladding
and punched out of the sheets high
under its gable
a message in dark empty holes, USE GAS.

*

Something's decided
to narrate
in more dimensions than I can know
the gathering in
and giving out of the world on a slow
pulse, on a metered contraction
that the senses enquire towards
but may not themselves
intercept. All I can tell it by
is the passing trace of it
in a patterned agitation of

a surface that shows only
metaphors. Riddles. Resemblances
that have me in the chute
as it meshes in closer, many modes
funnelling fast through one event,
the flow-through so
dense with association
that its colour comes up, dark
brownish green, soaked and
decomposing leaves
in a liquor.

*

And the biggest of all the apparitions,
the great iron
thing, the ironworks,
reared up on end into the bright
haze, makes quiet burning
if anything at all.

When the pulse-beat for it comes
it is revealed, set
back a little way, arrested,
inward, grotesque, prepared for.

Then gone by,
with the shallowing of the road
and the pulse's falling away
cleanly through a few more
frames of buildings, noise,
a works gate with cyclists;
the passing of it quite final, not a tremor
of the prospect at the crossroads;
open light, green paint on a sign,
the trolley wires
chattering and humming from somewhere else.

1 Calling

Waiting in blood. Get out of the pit.
That is the sign for parting. Already
the world could be leaving us.

*

Ancient
face-fragments of holy saints
in fused glass, blood-red and blue,
scream and stare and whistle
from where they're cobbled
into a small
new window beside the Dee;

trapped and raving
they pierce the church wall
with acids, glances of fire and lenses out of the light
that wanders under the trees and around
the domed grave-cover
lichened the colour of a duck's egg.

A pick-handle or a boot
long ago freed them
to do these things;
or what was
flung as a stone,
having come slowly on
out of a cloudiness in the sea.

*

Late at night
as the house across the street
stands rigid to the wind
and the lamp on its concrete column plays

static light on to it
everything writhes
through the unstable overgrown philadelphus
covering the whole end wall, its small heart-leaves
flickering into currents that
rock across the wall diagonally upward
and vanish, pursued, white
blossom-packs plucked at hard
and the tall stems
swirled to and fro, awkward
in the floods of expression.

A year or two past the gale
I walk out of the same door
on a night when I have
no depth. Neither
does the opposed house,

the great bush,
glory of the wall, sawn back
for harbouring insurrection and ghosts.

Now nothing
the whole height of the brickwork
to intercept expression.

– You'll know this ten-yard stretch
of suburban tarmac, where something
shakes at you; this
junction-place of back lanes, rutted gullies
with half a car
bedded in half a garage,
this sudden fence-post that breaks step;

the street, the chemist's shop, the lamp;

a stain in the plaster that so
resembles – and that body of air
caught between the ceiling
and the cupboard-top, that's like
nothing that ever was.

      *

A tune
is already a metaphor
and a chord
a metaphor wherein
metaphors meet.

      *

Wastes of distant darkness
and a different wind
out of the pit
blasts over a desolate
village on the outskirts
after midnight. Driving fast
on peripheral roads
so as to be repeatedly elsewhere
I pick up out of the blackness
waving torches, ahead and
over to one side.

And they are white, and lilac,
lemonade, crimson, magenta,
dull green;

festive little bulbs
strung between poles, left out
to buck and flail, rattling
all night,
                receding as I go,
the last lights,
the only lights.
The sign they make as I pass
is ineluctable
disquiet. Askew. The sign, once there,
bobbing in the world,
rides over intention, something
let through in error.

                *

Sudden and grotesque
callings. Grown man
without right learning; by nobody
guided to the places; not knowing
what might speak; having eased awkwardly
into the way of being called.

                *

In the places,
on their own account, not
for anybody's comfort:
gigantic peace.

Iron walls
tarred black, and discoloured,
towering in the sunlight
of a Sunday morning on
Saltley Viaduct.

Arcanum. Forbidden
open space, marked out with
tramlines in great curves among blue
Rowley Rag paving bricks.

Harsh reek in the air
among the monstrous squat
cylinders puts it
beyond doubt. Not a place
for stopping and spying.

The single human refuge
a roadside urinal, rectangular
roofless sarcophagus of tile and brick,
topped round with spikes and
open to the sky.

      *

The few moments in the year when the quadruped
rears on its hindlegs to mount,
foreparts and head
disconnected, hooves dangling,
the horned head visibly not itself;
but something.

      *

Waiting in blood.
The sign for parting. The straight way forward
checks, turns back
and sees it has passed through,
some distance back and without knowing it,
the wonderful carcass,
figurehead or spread
portal it was walking,
walking to be within;

showing from a little distance now its
unspeakable girdering, waste cavities,
defenceless structures in collapse; grey
blight of demolition without removal,
pitiable and horrific;

the look that came forward and through
and lit the way in.

      *

Gradbach Hill, long hog's back
stretching down west among taller hills
to the meeting of Dane river
with the Black Brook skirting its steeper side,
the waters joining
by Castor's Bridge, where the bloomery
used to smoke up into the woods
under the green chapel;
the hill,
stretching down west from Goldsitch
a mile from my side yard, shale measures
on its back and the low black spoilheaps
still in the fields,
darkens to an October sunset
as if it were a coal,
the sun sinking into Cheshire, the light
welling up slow along the hillside,
leaving the Black Brook woods
chill, but striking for a while
fire meadows out of red-brown soft-rush,
the dark base, the hollows, the rim swiftly
blackening and crusting over.

II The Return

Whatever breaks
from stasis, radiance or dark
impending, and slides
directly and fast on its way, twisting
aspect in the torsions of the flow
this way and that,
                    then suddenly
over,
        through a single
glance of another force touching it or
bursting out of it sidelong,

158

doing so
fetches the timeless flux
that cannot help but practise
materialisation,
the coming into sense,
to the guesswork of the senses,
the way in cold air
ice-crystals, guessed at, come densely
falling from where they were not;

and it fetches
timeless identities
riding in the flux with no
determined form, cast out of the bodies
that once they were, or out of
the brains that bore them;

but trapped into water-drops,
windows they glanced through
or had their images
detained by and reflected
or into whose molten glass the coloured oxides
burned their qualities;

like dark-finned fish embedded in ice
they have life in them that can be revived.

      *

There is ancient
and there is seeming ancient;
new, and seeming new –
venerable cancer, old as the race,
but so made as to bear
nothing but urgencies –

there is persuading the world's
layers apart with means
that perpetually alter and annex,
and show by the day what they can;

but still, with hardly a change to it,
the other dream or intention: of encoding
something perennial
and entering Nature thereby.

The masque for that
comes in its own best time
but in my place.

Bladelike and eternal, clear,
the entry into Nature
is depicted by
the vanishing of a gentleman
in black, and in portraiture,
being maybe a Doctor John
Dee, or Donne, or Hofmannsthal's
Lord Chandos,
                    he having lately walked
through a door in the air
among the tall
buildings of the Northern Aluminium Company
and become inseparable
from all other things, no longer
capable of being imagined
apart from them, nor yet of being
forgotten in his identity.

All of that is enacted
at the far top
of the field I was born in,

long slope of scrub, then pasture,
still blank on the map three hundred years
after the walkings of all such gentlemen
out of the air

then suddenly printed across with
this century, new, a single
passage of the roller
dealing out streets of terraces
that map like ratchet-strips, their gables
gazing in ranks above the gardens

at a factory sportsground,
a water-tower for steam-cranes, more
worksheds, and,
                    hulking along a bank
for a sunset peristyle, the long dark
tunnel-top roof of a football stadium.

All so mild, so late
in that particular change;
still seeming new.
                    Some of it,
my streets – Kentish Road,
Belmont, Paddington, Malvern –
just now caught up and lacquered
as Urban Renewal, halted
in the act of tilting to break up
and follow the foundries out
and the stamping mills,
the heavy stuff; short lives, all of them.

But still through that place
to enter Nature; it was possible,
it was imperative.

Something always
coming out, back against the flow,
against the drive to be in,
                    close to the radio,
the school, the government's wars;

the sunlight, old and still,
heavy on dry garden soil,

and nameless mouths,
events without histories, voices,
animist, polytheist, metaphoric,
coming through;

the sense of another world
not past, but primordial,
everything in it
simultaneous, and moving
every way but forward.

Massive in the sunlight, the old woman
dressed almost all in black, sitting out
on a low backyard wall,
rough hands splayed on her sacking apron
with a purseful of change in the pocket,
black headscarf tight across the brow, black
cardigan and rough skirt, thick stockings,
black shoes worn down;
                              this peasant
is English, city born; it's the last
quarter of the twentieth century
up an entryway
in Perry Barr, Birmingham, and there's
mint sprouting in an old
chimneypot. No imaginable
beginning to her epoch, and she's
ignored its end.

                    *

Timeless identities,
seeming long
like the one they called Achilles,
or short, like William Fisher,
age ten years, occupation, jeweller,
living in 1861 down Great King Street
in a household
headed by his grandmother, my ancestress
Ann Mason, fifty-seven, widow,
occupation, mangler; come in
from Hornton, back of Edge Hill,
where the masons were quarrying for Christminster.

                    *

These identities, recorded by authority
to be miniaturised; to be traceable
however small; to be material;
to have status in the record;
to have the rest,
the unwritten,
even more easily scrapped.

                    *

Mind
and language
and mind out of language again, and
language again and for ever

fall slack and pat
by defect of nature
into antinomies. Unless

thrown. And again
and repeatedly thrown
to break down the devil
his spirit; to pull down
the devil his grammar school,
wherein the brain
submits to be
cloven, up,
sideways and down
in all of its pathways;

where to convert
one term to its antithesis
requires that there be devised
an agent with authority –

and they're in. That's it. Who
shall own death? Spoken for,
and Lazarus the test case. Only Almighty
God could work that trick. Accept
that the dead have gone away to God through
portals sculpted in brass to deter,
horrific. The signs of it, passably
offensive in a cat or a herring,
in a man are made out
unthinkably appalling: *vide*
M. Valdemar's selfless
demonstration; drawn back and forth,
triumphantly racked in a passage without
extent, province of the agent,
between antithesis and thesis.

Sale and Lease-back. Perennial
wheeze. In the body's exuberance
steal it, whatever it is, sell it back again,
buy it in, cheap,
put it out to rent. If it's freedom, graciously
grant it,
                asking in return no more than
war service, wage-labour, taxes,
custodial schooling, a stitched-up
franchise. Trade
town futures for fields,
railroad food in, sell it on the streets.

And as if it were a military installation
specialise and classify and hide
the life of the dead.

                *

Under that thunderous
humbug they've been persistently
coming and going, by way of
the pass-and-return valve between the worlds,
not strenuous; ghosts
innocent of time, none the worse
for their adventure, nor any better;

that you are dead
turns in the dark of your spiral,
comes close in the first hours after birth,
recedes and recurs often. Nobody
need sell you a death.

                *

The ghosts' grown children
mill all day in the Public Search Office
burrowing out names for their own bodies, finding
characters with certificates but no
stories. Genetic behaviour,
scrabbling, feeling back across the spade-cut
for something; the back-flow of the genes'
forward compulsion suddenly
showing broken, leaking out, distressed.

164   *

They come anyway
to the trench,
the dead in their surprise,
taking whatever form they can
to push across. They've no news.
They infest the brickwork. Kentish Road
almost as soon as it's run up
out in the field, gets propelled
to the trench, the soot still fresh on it,

and the first few dozen faces
take the impress, promiscuously
with door and window arches;
Birmingham voices in the entryways
lay the law down. My surprise
stares into the walls.

III Authorities

If only the night can be supposed
unnaturally tall, spectrally
empty, and ready to disgorge
hidden authorities,
summonses, clarifications;

if it can be accorded pomp
to stretch this Grecian office-block
further up into the darkness, lamplit
all the way from the closed shopfronts
and growing heavier; then

that weight of attribution
jolts the entire thing down, partway
through its foundations, one corner heaving
into this panelled basement
where by the bar
the light spreads roseate and dusty.

If all that, then this,
ceiling sagged, drunk eyes
doing the things they do,
stands to be one of the several
cysts of the knowledge, distributed
unevenly through the middle of the mass;
if not, then not.

Brummagem conjuration
for the late Fifties. Not many
hypotheses in play then, even with the great
crust of brick and tarmac finally
starting to split and break up,
the dead weight of the old imperious
racket thrashing on
across its own canted-up wreckage.

Hard to be there, the place
unable to understand
even its own Whig history
for what it was; teachers
trained not to understand it
taught it, and it never fitted. Even less
did the history of the class struggle
reach down or along to the working-
class streets where work and wages
hid, as the most real shame.
                              – Don't
ask your little friend
what his father does;
don't let on we've found out
his mother goes to work;
don't tell anyone at all
what your father's job is.
If the teacher asks you
say you don't know.
                    Hard
to be still there. In the razings
and ripping of the slopes, the draining
away of districts, a quick irregular
stink of its creation coming through,
venerable, strong and foul.

*

Drawn to the places
by their oddness;
guided by nobody
to the subterranean
pea-green cafés,
the cafés in the style of lit
drains, the long plunging
high-walled walkway down
beside the railway viaduct
into moments that would
realign the powers if they could only
be distended;

sent by nobody,
meeting nobody
but the town gods.

The town gods are parodic,
innocent. They've not
created anything. Denizens.
Personages who keep strange hours,
who manifest
but are for the most part mute,

being appearances,
ringed eyes,
ikons designed to stare out
at the ikon-watcher, the studious
artisan walking in wait
at strange hours for the guard
to drop. Haunted
voyeur.

What could they ever say?
Wrecked people
with solitary trajectories,
sometimes rich clothing,
moving against the street currents
or lit from above, standing in bars;
always around the places
where the whores in the afternoon
radiate affront.

          If this were art
these beings could be
painted into the walls and released
from their patrolling.

          *

In the hierarchies, however disordered,
it would be warlords, kings and those
with the strength to usurp who went, clean,
to the disreputable, undeniable oracle
to have their own thoughts
twisted back in through their ears in style;

in the civilisation of novels,
the fields racked hard
to shake people off into suburbs
quiescent with masterless men
in their generations, it would be
pacifist mystics, self-chosen,
who would be driven by private
obsessions to go looking
among slurries and night-holes
for what might be accidentally
there, though not instituted; having to be
each his own charlatan.

          *

Grotesquely called,
grotesquely going in, fools
persisting in their folly,
all isolates, supposing
differently, finding differently: priests'
sons with dishevelled wits, teachers
with passed-on clothes and a little Homer,

a little Wordsworth, two or three
generations of Symbolist poets; compelled
by parody to insist
that what image the unnatural
law had been stamping
was moving into Nature,

and, once there,
could not but have its
orifices of question.

*

Sadist-voyeur,
stalled and stricken, fallen
into that way from the conviction of
not doing but
only looking;

nothing to be shot for,
forcibly drugged or even
set about in the free market
and kicked insensible;
invitations to conform, assumptions
of healing, animal sanity, left
to women's initiatives
in the style of the time; teachers
with slipped-off clothes, drawing back
the candlewick covers of the time,
jerking artistically,
letting faith pace observation.

*

If this were sanity and
sanity were art, this morning street
outside the old music shop would be
robustly done. Portrayal of the common
people and their commonplace bosses
with classless nostalgia. Courbet
transfigured into every substance of it;
every sensation that surrounds,
passes or emanates
entering the world in the manner of
telling or seeing; with no need
to be lifted by art out of
the nondescript general case because never
for a second inhabiting it; detectable
identities, of gear-shifts, stumblings, jackets,
coming through unimpeded.

*

Birmingham voice
hollow under the dark
arch of the entryway,

by slow torsion wrenched
out of her empty jaw, sunk
hole of lips; no way it could be
understood or answered.

The nearest people. Neighbour-fear
for the children, nine
inches of brick away
year after year from the beginning;

barren couple, the man desperate,
irascible, the woman
namelessly sick, tottering
in extremis for years, bald, spectral,
skin sunk from sallow
to sooty brown, wide eyes set
straight ahead, yellowing,
walking dead. Early

learning. And the dog,
dung-coloured whirl of hatred
too quick for a shape, never still,
slavering and shouting
to hurl itself against the garden
palings repeatedly. A welcome
for my first free steps among the flowers.
Slow-dying woman,
her life was primordial and total,
the gaze-back of the ikon; her death
modern and nothing, a weekend in the Cold War.
The dog must have brained itself.

Had the three of them been art, it would all have
been beaten pewter, dulling
in low relief,
              or the grey
sculpture-gibbet of an *enclos paroissial*,
exemplary figures of misery hobbled

to a god bent on confusion,
mercilessly modelled,
glistening when rained on.

His widowhood
was modern and quiet, his death
art: upright in his armchair in the daylight,
facing the door, his eyes
oddly narrowed and suspicious, just
as they were in his life.
He was silvered. It was done.

                    *

Once invented, the big city
believed it had a brain; Joe
Chamberlain's sense of the corporate
signalling to itself with millions of disposable
identity-cells, summary and tagged.

Right under all that, the whole
construction continued to seethe
and divide itself by natural law; not

into its tributary villages again,
but winning back Dogpool,
Nechells, Adderley Park and the rest

in the cause of a headless
relativity of zones, perceptible
by the perceiver, linked by back roads,

unstable, dividing, grouping again
differently; giving the slip to being
counted, mapped or ever recognised
by more than one head at a time.

Vigilant dreaming head
in search of a place to lay itself.

IV Core

Dead acoustic.

Dead space.

Chamber with no echo
sits at the core, its place
plotted by every force. Within,
a dead fall.

Grave-goods that have motion
have it on their own account,
respond to nothing.
The chamber whose location knots
an entire symmetry
uses none.

Heterogeneous,
disposed without rhythm,
climax, idiom or generic law,

grave goods send word back out.

*

That sky-trails may merge with earth-trails,
the material spirits
moving in rock as in air,

it's down by just a step or two
into the earth, mounded above at the sky,

and the floor obliquely
tilting a little
to the upper world again.

We're carving the double spiral
into this stone; don't
complicate or deflect us.
We know what we're at.

We're letting the sun perceive
we've got the hang of it.

Write sky-laws into the rocks; draw
the laws of light into it and through it.

On the door under the ground
have them face inwards
into what might otherwise seem dark.

                    *

Inside a total stillness
as if inside the world but nowhere
continuous with it,

a warehouse with blocked
windows, brickwork and staging
done matt black
and cleverly lit to resemble
a warehouse
put to night uses;

suspended in there, moving
only on its own account,
the image, *deus mortuus*,
death chuckling along in its life,
uncanny demonstration, one edge
of clowning, charlatan,
the other huskily
brushing against nothing,

in the outermost arm of the spiral,
where it disintegrates,
gives itself up, racing
to flake away,

he is once again passing
close to his birth; Hawkins
on his last go-round,

declining solids, genially
breaking apart, brown man

with papery skin
almost as grey as his
beard and long hair,
the look of a hundred winters
down on his shrunk shoulders

that shake with a mysterious
mutter and chuckle across the mouthpiece,
private, bright-eyed, hung
light in his jacket, shuffling
on wrecked legs,
the old
bellow, the tight leathery sound
shredded, dispersed,

the form of a great force
heard as a monstrously amplified
column of breath, with
scribbles of music across it.

*

Without motion, or sign of motion,
or any history of it,
a polished black basalt
pyramid, household size.

Reflective hornblende faces, wedges
that seem ageless but not old;

here flown as fugitive
from all exegesis.

*

Peachy light
of a misty late afternoon
strokes, with some difficulty
for all they're above ground, the bared
cheekbones of certain villagers;

has to get round
the bulk of St Fiacre

and through the tall open stone-framed
window-spaces of the modest lean-to
ossuary by the wall;

and has to
pick them out in there
from among shovels, vases,
wheelbarrows, watering-cans;
and go in to them by
their personal windows.

They're on a shelf,
the last half-dozen or so,
up out of the way,

housed in a style
between hatbox and kennel,
tin, or matchwood, painted
black, painted pale green,

skull-patterned,
lettered, *Chef de M.* ———,
Chef de Mlle.———, and dated. First
quarter, twentieth century.

*

Over on Barnenez headland
the long stepped cairn
heavily drawn
across the skyline
has itself seen to be on watch,

powerfully charged
with the persons of certain
translated energies,

the wall of masonry courses
spiked with them, passages,
a bank of ovens in a tilery,
their dispositions
by no means symmetrical;

their buried radiance
variable, heavily shielded,
constantly active; of fearsomely
uncertain mood and
inescapable location.

v **Colossus**

The scheme
of Adolphe Sax

that there should be
a giant presence in the sky

rearing above Paris,
slung between four
towers taller than Notre Dame;

blaring into the rain,
a vast steam organ
in the style of the technology and the time,
its truck-sized player-cylinders fed to it
by locomotives;
                         all found in the heart
and its logic, just as Piranesi found
what was appalling but unbuilt.

Le Notre, L'Enfant
surfaced closer to the possible.
Paris was spared
the sight of the colossus
rising in a forest of sticks, the way
sections of Liberty in the foundry-yard
towered behind the houses,

and also the inevitable doom of it, cannonaded,
rusted and sagging, enormous
broken image of the Siege.

       *

And up comes the Grand Fleet
from the floor of Scapa Flow,

pale-bellied, featureless, decomposing,
bloated with pumped air,

breaking the grey surface, hulk after hulk,
huge weight of useful iron

slithered across, cut into,
sold off: worn tanks of fire

that trundled through the sea,
both sides' dirty coal-smoke
blown the same way in battle.

      *

Clarity
of the unmoving core
comes implacably out
through all that's material:

walls of battleship scrap,
the raising up of Consett
along the skyline,
the taking of it down again.

      *

Mansions of manufacturers strung along ridges
upwind of prosperity built in infernal
images below,
                well out of it, but not yet
out of sight.
            Were they
mansions in Paradise, looking out over Hell?
Were they mansions in the better parts of Hell?

Question evaded by the model
chief residences of the model factories,
set upon slight
elevations of the Middle Way.

      *

This age has a cold blackness of hell
in cities at night. London
is filled with it, Chicago cradles it
in ice-green glitter along
the dark of the lake. Birmingham Sparkbrook,
Birmingham centre, Birmingham Castle Vale
hang in it as holograms. For now

Puritan materialism dissolves its matter,
its curdled massy acquisition; dissolves
the old gravity of ponderous fires
that bewildered the senses,
                              and for this
glassy metaphysical void.

Something will be supposed
to inhabit it, though it is not
earth, sky or sea. There will be
spastic entrepreneurial voyages twitched out
from wherever its shores may lie.

                    *

Mercurial nature with a heaviness to it
flies with an eye to sitting
down somewhere and being serious.

With a heaviness to it, an opacity
saddening its flight.

Haunted look of stalled energy, of rights
impatiently or contemptuously surrendered.

VI The Many

Transit of Augusta Treverorum
to Trier; a location
busy with evolutionary forms long
before the brain-birth of 1818.

First, a grid-city, fit to support Constantine's
huge palace and basilica, working
as it was designed to do, its defences
anchored to bastions;
the size and operation
generating the structures of the first rank.

The size vanished; the operation
ceased. On all sides
the general case
collapsed, and the nettles grew out of it,

and the beasts fed there and let fall
their dung. There will have been scrub,
and mounds, and the rest of the new
general case of reversion,

out of which still rose up
spaced widely and without relation, certain
of the great masonry contraptions
that gave no proper
account of how they'd been arrived at.

Next, the shelter of each of those things
generated a settlement of scufflers,
scratchers of livings. Pragmatic
tracks linked one with another; in due time
the separate nuclei touched their
forces together and fused

to a mediaeval city which, conceived,
closed off. It walled what it was. It sat

smaller than the Roman city, quite
differently shaped
and oriented; entirely grown
out of the landmarks of that city,
and ignorant of it.

I see such things worked rapidly,
in my lifetime; hard for the body to believe in.

*

Mercurial nature, travelling fast,
laterally in broken directions, shallow,
spinning, streaked out in separate lights, an
oil film dashed on a ripple,
its plural bands
drawn out and tonguing back on themselves,

in an instant is gone
vertically on a plunge, on a sudden
switch of attitude,
                              without ever
pausing to drop its flight,
compose itself, gain weight;
                                        dives
narrowly deep, as far down
as anything;
                    plunges unaltered,
slips away down
in twisted filaments, separable
argumentative lights.

                    *

Parable of the One and the Many. Presences
flaring out from the wet flints
at Knowlton ruin,

multiple as beans, too small and irregular
to distinguish or call names. Divide;
survive.
              Some god, isolated
by a miscalculation, cut off
from his fellows, hauled in
across the bank to clear the green
ring of its demons; churched over;
and in his time forsaken.

They ate him,
and drank him,
and put his little light out and left.

                    *

The stones are waters
the stones are fires
dragged in a swirl across the core,

these slopes their after-image
fixed into the longest
fade they can secure;

ice, and sunlight, and blackened
crusts, lichen and heather sweeps
tilting off, one through another.

Draining through peat-hags,
Dane River, by its weight sucked out
from a mile of upland bog

to pour down, stained
through a crumbling, matt-black, moist
ravine of soft, firm

stuff that could be fire;
peat scattered with coal glitter,
mineshafts in a trail before

the drop into pastures.
These moorlands
hang down in swags from the sky,

from graves in the sky,
companies of lives lifted up;
Stanton Moor, Knot Low,

Shutlingsloe,
tilted, eroded cone,
mutable, as the lands turn on it,

as if it were a cloud shape
or the massing of a mood, emerging
to be directly read.

Over away from Dane
Axe Edge sends down the Dove,
gathers the Manifold

and lets it slip
through complexity;
the hills in their turns tantalise

and instruct, then the learning
dissolves. There's no
holding it all. Steadily

as the star-fields swing by,
this land-maze
brushes against, and stirs

somnolent body-tracks, unmapped
traces in the brain.
Axe Edge

thrust up towards the anvil-cloud
full of rivers, the skyline
inky and dark. Under

the evening, the hoof-strike flashes.

*

Landscape superimposed
upon landscape. The method
of the message lost
in the poetry of Atlantis
at its subsiding to where all
landscapes must needs be
superimpositions on it. All landscapes
solid, and having transparency
in time, in state. Odysseus old –
what to do with him?
– sent out to have his hardened
senses touch against lost reality.
It is called water that he passes through.

*

The boys are swinging firecans
along through the dusk;

rusty cans, bodged with holes,
with long string handles, coals from the grate

and whistled through oxygen to make
red-eyed pepperpots, clustered

fire-points, raging away in a trail
of acrid chimney smoke in the street.

*

The land, high and low,
has been scattered across with fire-pots;
brick, iron, lidded, open to the sky,
the glare streaming upward
in currents and eddies of sparks, blackening
the look of the rim, the district,
even by day, requiring that it be
strong; that it shall one day split itself

*

The true gods, known only
as *those of whom there is never news;*

rebellious, repressed; indestructible
right access to the powers of the world;

by tyrannies given images; given
finish, given work; and in due time

discarded among the debris of that into
private existences, into common use,

deliquescent, advancing by a contrary
evolution to the giving up of all

portrayable identity, seeping unevenly
down to a living

level, pragmatic
skein of connections from

lichens to collapsing faces
in drenched walls, exhalations

of polish and detergent
in palace-voids of authority,

patches of serene light in the skulls of
charlatans making tea in swamp cottages,

evidences that dart into the particle accelerator
unaccountably; and others

caught unawares in the promiscuous
rectangles of the Impressionists,

and ready to come back out to us
through the annexation-frames
of a world that thought itself a single colony.

                    *

Coming home by the road across Blackshaw Moor
in a summer dawn with the ridge just showing
grey above the plain and out of the white mist;

a red eye goggling high in the dark rocky
crest of Hen Cloud, a lamp in crimson canvas
up there somewhere. That skyline
was mad enough already.

                    *

One particular of Poseidon: the bronze statue
through whose emptied eyeholes
entire Poseidon comes and goes.

VII On Fennel-Stalks

They have no choice but to appear.

We knew they existed, but not what they'd be like;
this visitation is the form that whatever

has been expected but not imaged takes
for the minutes it occupies now.
                              Just after sunset,
looking out over the thin snow,
the moor vegetation, stiff canopy,
showing through it, greying. Wind
getting up, dragging smoky cloud-wisps
rapidly across on a line
low in the sky.
                       Another wind,
steady and slow from the north, freezing
and far higher; and with it,
rising from behind the ridge, gigantic
heads lifted and processing along it, sunset-lit,
five towering beings
looking to be miles high,
their lower parts hidden, their lineaments
almost stable in their infinitely slow
movement.
                    Relief at the sight of them
even though they seem to mean
irrevocable dislocation. Creatures
of the Last Days, coming to the muster.

Apocalypse
lies within time; as these beings
may or may not so lie; if they do,
their demeanour could equally match
the beginning of all things. It's the same
change. There's a choice of how to see it.

For them, no such choice. Self-generated,
and living perfect to themselves
in some other dimension, they have it
laid on them to materialise in the cold
upper air of the planet;
and arriving there
they can take on only the shapes
the terms of materialisation impose.

Visibly not as they would wish to be,
they're self-absorbed. The human eye

watches them shrewdly, albeit
with the awe it's been craving; sizes them up,
how to ride them.

*

Cargo-cult
reversed. There have always been
saucers put out for us
by the gods. We're called
for what we carry.

In barbarous times
all such callings
come through as rank parodies,

refracted by whatever murk
hangs in the air;
even the long pure
sweep of the English pastoral
that stretched its heart-curve
stronger, and more remarkably wide

merely to by-pass
the obstruction caused by a burst
god, the spillage
staining the economic imperative
from end to end with divinity.

*

Mythos,
child of action, mother of action;

hunger for action understands itself
only by way of its own

secretion, fluid metaphysical carrier
that makes, where it collides, cultures,

and where it runs free, myth,
child of action, mother of action.

*

There can be quaint cultures
where a poet who incurs exile
will taste it first,
                    puzzling half a life
at the statues in the town park and those
particular shin-high railings there;

afterwards, fame and disgrace.

Succeeding a single blink of passage
through a beam of power
on the road between fortunes; between
province and metropolis,
art and art, fantasy
and amenity.

                    *

The snails of Ampurias
ascend
          as the canopy of air
upon the ruins
cools after sunset.

They infest
                    the wild fennel
that infests the verges of the road
through what have become wide
spaces above the bay.

The snails ascend
                    the thin clear light,
taking their spirals higher;
                              in the dusk
luminous white, clustered
like seed-pods of some other plant;

quietly
rasping their way round
                              together, and upward;
tight and seraphic.

NOTES

PAGE 158: *Gradbach Hill*. In North-West Staffordshire close to Three Shires Head, where Derbyshire, Cheshire, and Staffordshire meet. Facing it across the Black Brook is the rocky cleft called Lud's Church, a place whose supposed connection with the composition of *Gawain and the Green Knight* I am willing to believe in.

PAGE 159: *'Like dark-finned fish...'* etc. Quoted from J. C. Powys, *Maiden Castle* (Macdonald, 1937).

PAGE 163: *M. Valdemar*. Suspended for months on end in the moment of death, in Poe's story.

PAGE 175: *Barnenez*. Ancient tumulus on the Kernéléhen peninsula in Brittany, no great distance from the village of St Fiacre.

PAGE 177: The German Grand Fleet surrendered at Scapa Flow after the First World War, and was then scuttled by its crews. Pictures of the raising of the ships were some of the most awesome images I saw in childhood.

PAGE 178: *The brain-birth of 1818*. The brain was Karl Marx's.

PAGE 180: *Knowlton*. In Dorset. An abandoned Christian church stands in the ring of an enclosure previously sacred to earlier deities whose ground it was tactically sent to occupy.

PAGE 181: *Axe Edge*. In Derbyshire, and reaching down to Three Shires Head. Within a mile or so of one another, on or under Axe Edge, rise three rivers: the Dane, flowing west into Cheshire, the Dove, flowing east, and the Manifold, running close to the Dove and eventually joining it.

PAGE 184: *Blackshaw Moor, Hen Cloud*. An upland plain in North-West Staffordshire and a crag overlooking it.

PAGE 187: *Ampurias*. Extensive Celtiberian, and later Roman, mercantile settlement in Catalonia.

NEW & UNCOLLECTED POEMS

(1996)

FROM The Dow Low Drop

When the far bank darkens
and the river starts to die
the nondescript
silently fights for its life

*

So out of what materials
shall we be making
our nothing?

There had been
nothing made. No
yet about it. No suggestion
something was bound
to come about; that nothing
could then have pictures done of it,
and very like. True nothing
needs hands to build its many forms.

There had been made
that which was nothing.

So now out of what
materials. Something
harvested, woven, bleached. Or
harvested, pulped
bleached and pressed.

Or chosen for pallor in the ground,
quarried, sawn into straight
sheets, polished;

breathed, even, as a cloud from some
temperature manoeuvre. All
edged with particular tastes.

Is the Mother
back from the mine? White-eyed
out of the footrail, having all afternoon

given shape to certain débris,
certain chunks; having been
final on matters
that offered themselves in darkness
under the birch-scrub slope.

*

Made from whatever material, the blank
skin announces no show.

Empty time.

When it puckers and punctures it slits
straight-mouthed, behaves
as a reversed letter-slot. Almost
everything that tumbles out
is furniture and the like, lived with
but not digested: sideboard,
ironing tackle, things for the kitchen
that match, air-fresheners, seersucker
sheets, candlewick covers,
mugs that match, all
the colours of crispbread; oldish
damp towels, heaters, the mail;
the sweat and push
to sustain all that
through a winter that won't end.

*

Aphrodite from the sky
fallen in Asia
black,
ferried to the island, a sacred
lumpish cone,
smaller than women,

raises the dead and
walks them for a while
without explaining.

My schoolmate, D.,
forty-seven years hanged,
parks the same rented car
as mine directly beside it,
lopes into the courtyard, makes
for the cool museum hall
where she sits, the landlady,
hiked out of shrine-rubble
and dusted down.

He's aged
just as he had to: same
chicken-legged gait, in shorts;
same haircut, grey; grown
the only moustache he could have,
gained a small wife.
And he just might be by now
German or Danish.

He's quieter. A good
career in a science behind him
following a narrow squeak in youth.

I could greet him, dull idea,
if I didn't believe my knowledge.

Died at fifteen, in his delight
alone in the house,
clothes-line over the banister,
mother's underwear – fine
calculation, could have been finer:
too much buzz. The censors of the day
comforted the boys with *suicide,
impatience, despair, tragedy*. Said
nothing about the underwear.

Hanging yourself's man's work.

*

Not only in desert cliffs,
rock-fares of affront,
cities of single rooms
piled along ravines,

but from afternoon shadows
and the crevices of seats by night
there's a wonderful
growl to be heard.

*

Go along and over the level last ridge of the Staffordshire mud-
stone above Longnor, and the limestone starts up at you from the
Dove, a ragged barricade of tall crooked points and green humps.
The turnpike dives, kinks to cross the river by lost Soham. *Vasta
est.* Far enough north to be harried. The manors along the Dove
wasted, then, after King William's days of deep speech, listed.
Beyond the river the road heads up through the barrier, on the bed
of the vanished feeder stream that tapped and emptied the shallow
sea's last lagoon. On the rocks at the grassy lake floor's edge I'm
living, in a house built as a publican's retreat. And across the lake
The Waste Called Dowlamore rises high and quick to the first true
edge of the limestone upland, the skyline that joins Hind Low,
Brier Low, Dow Low, Hoard Low. Illusion, the set tilted with its
bushes, walls and crossing cows, and cutting off at the sky where
the National Park stops dead also, fresh out of scenery. There's no
backside to Dow Low. A straight cut, quarried down hundreds of
feet to the floor below base level: the immense abyss of jobs. From
the rim, a view over all the fields to the east, greened with their
own dug lime, seethed in their mother's milk, cratered at Tun-
stead, Dove Holes, Topley Pike with more prints of New Eleusis.

Epic

'Stranger, in your own land
how do men call you?'

'I will tell you. Men call me Roy
Fisher. Women call me
remote.'

Stop

Spent all his life
playing for time.
All of it.

A Modern Story
A prophecy (1981)

Being past fifty, with suspiciously few enemies
and just about enough achievements

I was sat in my garden, watching over my grey peas,
when there came to me – not in a flash, but more like

a sunken boiler, slowly and implacably surfacing of its own
volition – the finest of all my ideas! It felt even then

as though it might be one of the five best
projects for a literary work in England at that moment

and, do you know, I was right! The Arts Council Literature Panel
awarded it one of their five bursaries: seven and a half thousand
        pounds I got.

But when the cheque came it gave me Writer's Block. Four days.
Five. Six. After a week, I no longer knew myself.

In what I can only call now a fit of distraction
I – founded a Poetry Competition, with my bursary money as the
        prize.

Though mad, I was canny, mind. I first sold my elder son
my project, cash down, to pay for the ads.

Then everything suddenly got very fast. Thirty-two thousand entries
came in at one pound fifty a time. That's forty-eight grand

and a handling problem. To help with the mail
and the critical rough sorting I was able to take on

four unemployed Ph.Ds and three newly-redundant
publishers' editors under the Government

Work Experience Scheme, and to give my younger son
a Youth Opportunity. And when it came to hiring the judges

I asked a few friends I valued for their fairness and cynicism
to guess who they'd inevitably be. It warmed my heart

to be able to prove them right. Then, three weeks before closing date,
I saw how I could use my Small Business Starter Allowance to
        double the prize money,

and that announcement brought in a late crop of entries, six
thousand or more. There were no problems

such as the judges giving one another the prizes; they gave them
to next year's judges as it turned out, but nobody knew that at
        the time.

So: with part of my fifty grand profits, and the unstoppable weapon
of thirty-eight thousand stamped addressed envelopes targeted on
poets,

I quickly put in a bid for a chain of South Coast vanity presses
that had overreached themselves and needed the gas bill paying.

At which point an easy-voiced man telephoned and asked to see me
'about England'.
I thought he was the Inland Revenue and invited him round with
caution.

He was tall, very affable, a little cold – Anthony Bate could have
played him:
his conversation was light, oblique and wide-ranging.

He gave the impression of a man in some way *authorised*
yet there was something in his drift that was erotic

though in no way you could specify. At length I was seized by the
idea
that, while taking care not in so many words to say it,

he was proposing to sell off to me, very cheap,
for me and my friends to do whatever we wanted with, a piece of
England

the Arts Council Literature Department! The staff. The files. The
goodwill.
He leaned back, and looked into my eyes. The figures took me only a
second

'No deal,' I told him. 'I'm a straight business man now, not a
gangster.'
He gave me his card. I presented him with one of my books,
edition of two thousand, remaindered.

It Follows That

1

Mainly what
hurts the mind: a few idylls
protected in it. Times
where there's no term
for *might-have-been,*
may even yet, elsewhere, then.

'Go on.' I won't

2

The car fights into the wind
along the moor top. Keeping pace
at a run and hidden by the dry stone walls,
the eternal unseen crow-flinger
shows what he still can do.

3

Last thing I want to do is invent something, particularly a building or a structure of any sort. It's a risk.

A fetish without the power to excite! Turning up. Hanging about. Floating in.

I could do with being restrained from inventing an opaque liturgy. With brass mountings.

If I were to invent a groin, maybe it wouldn't stay. They have a tendency to be moving off – *There* you are! Behaviour! Conduct. Coming and going. The swim. And it's away. Narrow squeak.

4

Medium-sized town
will do. Filled with nuisance,
clothing, bedding, bores.
Every last thing in it
loose as the day it arrived;
flying past my ear but not
leaving.

5

So much gone. Recollections of it
posters of the present
papering rooms the gales yank.

6

Began to sleep. And soon in sleep came
Work; System with ivory lips
nostrils and ears; Forgetfulness
forever startled into remembering.

And the new place, learned rapidly before erasure:
loose treads, warm corner, how
to wash and conceal your cup.

7

Crushed phials and muddy patches of a winter
where a membrane not laminated
peels itself apart
to a pair of split skins
their inner surfaces
bared to the light of a Spring
that creaks like Doomsday,
rears up to dry, all promise, no more
running back home. Habitual
broad-nosed walk on the ring road
by the cleared-out brassica field,
ticking past medallioned railings

to where they corner to cage in
a sodden unnameable black
bole, sawn off
so low it sprawls into a beast.

8

There is a wallpaper,
dusty-patterned, faded red-brown on
faded yellow, the back
of an old playing card.

Shut in with the pattern, you can ride it,
feel it lift off, made ready. Then
It will proceed to move undeniably
through time, shuttling
forward and back with experimental
conviction. In themselves the journeys
show nothing.

9

How the hotel
can ever expand to imagine itself –
lodged, an oracular shell,
in the curve of the Square
where a statue rises over the toilets,
and dedicated steadily to Change. One
public entrance and one only.
A limited range of deals going on.
But the idea of the place,
roofless, chaotic, infinite.

10

Hulk
slides down the night
sky in a strong
forward descent. As good
as finished. There've been no
onboard warning lights. And the monster
never had a self to be sorry for.

11

In brooding,
balance, pleasure,
power. Brooding is voiceless
image stored with no bodily
trace; recoverable only by
strenuous and dense
translation. I don't like writing.

12

Under the wet
mountain at sundown,
the small mountain,
dark, a burnt cone,
December holding the ash-poles
separate and cold,

I'm talking in the water,
slender runs from the sky
into glass panels
and sidelong out. Small
mountain sits in the valley floor,
on the water in the soil,
black pyramid of absence, tilted
fields outlined on the dark.

All the fingers of a hand
grip, twist and with
the fingers of another, wring
the soak-water out,
running on the asphalt strip
that hikes a sky-glint
over the river.

What's
been the sun, sliding all day
unseen above the cloud-lid,
gleams without form from a gap
at the horizon; gleams
a long while, picking up water.

13

Thinking straight thoughts
year in year out
shortens the temper. Bending
the world brings bliss
somewhere the other slde of
boredom at having to bend so.

14

Scratched in the plaster where the wallpaper peels:

The lean years follow the years of need —
they write, that will not read —
St Priapus be our speed!

15

Maybe there's been
a new moon. Visible
from the Pennine edge, far off
across the whole dark plain of Cheshire,
a huge curved horn, glowing yellow,
rears over Merseyside
and draws itself in.

If it's the moon, good.

Hand-Me-Downs

The nineteenth century of the bizarre
system of dates the Christians have
stands almost empty. Everybody
who helped design the first of the World
Wars is dead, no longer doing much
to anybody; likewise most of the begetters
and settlers-up of the next. They've got
clean away. And so on.

Turnips, four short rows, but enough.
Potatoes, plenty. Kale. For surplus
baby tomatoes, a jar with olive oil
an inch deep over the fruit,
then topped off with aqua vitae,
to rest on the oil and guard it. And
seal tight. And look forward
to winter. Ordinary life,
'restorable' 'normal' 'life' – paraffin,
pepper, fingers that stroke and grip –
sits in the brain like the supreme contemptuous
coinage of disease, nothing more
than a counter devised for murderers to bargain with.

The Slink

Round behind Harecops and up across Archford Moor,
a slope of hedged fields with a road up or down.
Zone of a few dozen acres. No focus: instead,
the appearance of being inclined to judge. The
judgement, understated.

Helpless awareness, wholly alert. Having the
discomfort, day and night, of a thread of language
passing through, pulled against it, reversed, re-
run; never breaking, never belonging.

Borne constantly over to one side, to the shelter
not of primary buildings – opera-house, cathedral,
law-palace, prison – but of the blankness of the
bare ground artists didn't render by more than a
wash and a few spacing figures who rummage there
or float, as the sun goes down and pediments shove
shadows.

Constantly to the left, as far as the isolated row
of shops, beached tram. *Saltender's*: boarded up
and the boards kicked in. *Cliff's*: incinerated,
the painted woodwork squared into satiny black
scales. *Adward's*: empty, a dump.

Just beyond night-fire's limits, burnt fur.

Seized slowly from the left: trapezius gives up
on the body, shapes only for itself. Locks off
the ribs, winds tighter with each step. Stops off
walking straight.

Index of titles and first lines
(titles are in italics, first lines in roman type)